Happy Birthday to my best &
friend Gale on her 50th birthday —
May we live a long and healthy 50
more years.
        Love,
        Linda

50

CELEBRATE

50

fifty extraordinary women talk about facing, turning, and being fifty

WRITTEN BY CONNIE COLLINS

Meredith® Books ▷ Des Moines, Iowa

More® Books
An imprint of Meredith® Books
Fifty Celebrate Fifty

Project Editor: Hilary Black
Writer: Connie Collins
Senior Associate Design Director: Richard Michels
Photography Editor: Lisa Burroughs
Copy Chief: Terri Fredrickson
Editorial Operations Manager: Karen Schirm
Managers, Book Production: Pam Kvitne, Marjorie J. Schenkelberg
Contributing Copy Editor: Jane Woychick
Contributing Proofreaders: Becky Danley, Gretchen Kauffman, Susan J. Kling
Research Coordinator: Kim Schulman
Electronic Production Coordinator: Paula Forest
Editorial and Design Assistants: Kaye Chabot, Mary Lee Gavin

Meredith® Books
Editor in Chief: James D. Blume
Design Director: Matt Strelecki
Managing Editor: Gregory H. Kayko
Executive Editor, New Business: Dan Rosenberg

Director, Sales, Special Markets: Rita McMullen
Director, Sales, Premiums: Michael A. Peterson
Director, Sales, Retail: Tom Wierzbicki
Director, Book Marketing: Brad Elmitt
Director, Operations: George A. Susral
Director, Production: Douglas M. Johnston
Vice President, General Manager: Douglas J. Guendel

More® Magazine
Editor in Chief: Myrna Blyth
Editor: Susan Crandell
Creative Director: Anna Demchick

Meredith Publishing Group
President, Publishing Group: Stephen M. Lacy
Vice President, Publishing Director: Bob Mate

Meredith Corporation
Chairman and Chief Executive Officer: William T. Kerr
Chairman of the Executive Committee: E. T. Meredith III

celebrate

50 50 50

{contents}

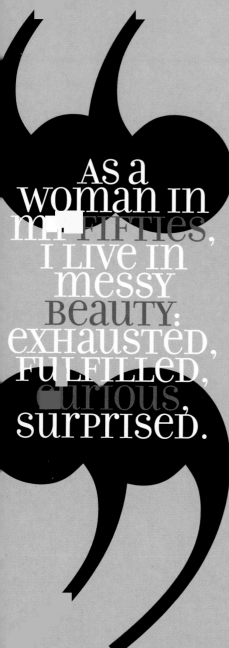

As a woman in my fifties, I live in messy beauty: exhausted, fulfilled, curious, surprised.

"I am not afraid of storms, for I am learning how to sail my ship."

A friend shared these words of Louisa May Alcott with me, soon after I finished filming *Little Women.* I have kept them with me ever since. Few other statements express as beautifully the way I view this particular time in my life. At 50, I could hoist my sail and move into the wind and sea with a kind of confidence and clarity I never had before—and that feeling has been nothing less than empowering.

As the new millennium dawns, we who have blossomed into middle age do not have to prove ourselves the way our counterparts in previous generations once did. Today, we can be women more fully. Physically, we can revel in the way that our faces tell the stories of our lives; while sexuality once was equated entirely with youth, the concept now has broadened to encompass maturity and experience. Emotionally, we are no longer expected to recede into the sidelines; instead, we can expand and rejoice in the richness of our lives, our work, and our families. Spiritually, we have learned how to regard life in a less linear way, and now we are able to embrace complexity and contradictions more fully.

For me, there's something so liberating about this stage of life. It's not that you know more, necessarily; it's that you accept not knowing and experience a different kind of ease. A woman's journey is one of constant discovery. Part of what I've discovered is that much of the beauty and mystery of this life can be found in the process of seeking.

{Fore

I'm in love with my life right now. Of course, that doesn't necessarily mean things are in any kind of order! Like millions of other women, I'm always tired and never seem to have enough time to accomplish everything I want. It's often difficult to get to one kid's baseball game, another's play, and the third's concert—while still being a loving partner, a good actor, and an attentive friend. Years ago, I might have punished myself for not doing and being enough. I know now that there is no perfect balance, no smooth, wrinkle-free way to pack it all in. Part of maturing is knowing that you're always making choices; something's got to give, so you just hope it's the least important thing. As a woman in my fifties, I live in messy beauty: exhausted, fulfilled, curious, surprised. The joy is in knowing that, each

WORD}

BY SUSAN SARANDON

"A woman's journey is one of constant discovery."

I HAVE LEARNED THAT WE SHOULD NEVER SETTLE FOR SOMEONE ELSE'S DEFINITION OF WHO WE CAN BE.

morning, there are a million reasons to get up and face the day.

My life has always been characterized by the unexpected, and I have always equated my personal growth with the ability to turn the unknown into commitment and fulfillment. I fell into my career; as I look back, I realize I'm grateful that it grew and developed when I was old enough to handle it. Professionally, I now know a confidence and authority I never could have felt when I was younger. I've grown into my best roles, and, rather than look back with longing, I look forward to the choices my work opens up for me. Recently, I had the extraordinary experience of working on a film with my daughter, Eva. Watching her bloom professionally is a gift I never could have anticipated. It brought us even closer.

Motherhood was another unexpected event in my life. In my twenties, I was told that I wouldn't be able to bear children. When Eva, Jack, and Miles came along in my late thirties and early forties, I was delighted—not only by their arrival, but by the ways in which they changed me for the better. Motherhood, as it turned out, was easier than it might have been when I was younger. By the time my kids were born, I already had learned how to laugh at my weaknesses and view potential failures as just another step, stumble, skip.

Now, as I move through my fifties, I can be professional and domestic, creative and intellectual, patient and urgent. I have learned that we should never settle for someone else's definition of who we can be—and, by extension, we must never let our children settle. These days, young {Fore people are often pressured to forgo their dreams to gain economic stability. I always tell my kids: Don't be too stuck on one road; life may have more imagination than you do. I want to invite my children, all our children, to look at what they see, take it all in, and then make choices.

Risk-taking is also a part of staying true—and perhaps experience teaches us which risks are the most worthwhile. One of the best risks that I've taken was a trip to Nicaragua in 1984, during the contra war. The fighting was intense, and many said the region was too dangerous to visit. But I felt strongly that it was important to help people who were suffering. So, along with a wonderful group of women from all over the United States, I delivered cereal to day care centers and visited communities that had been ravaged by the conflict. The trip was sponsored by MADRE, a human rights organization that supports women's development in zones of conflict; the opportunity to meet and travel with women of different ages, from different experiences and backgrounds, ended up changing my life.

I've always felt that it is important to use my celebrity to promote the causes I believe in—and I've learned over the years how to do so while staying true to myself. Being a well-known person gives me both the ability and the responsibility to speak publicly for what I care about passionately, and to lend my voice to those whose own voices often are not heard. My work as an activist has opened my eyes and my heart by introducing me to some of the most important people in my life.

Part of reaching this age is really knowing yourself, and being able to get the most out of that knowledge. I've found that, for me, friends, family, and community are a lifeline. I try to surround myself with people who are passionate about what they do, people who are funny and curious and savvy. I love spending time with friends I've known for years; we've shared so many rites of passage. I get joy from women who, in their seventies and eighties, can kick up their heels and enjoy themselves. Without a sense of humor, we'd all wither up!

WORD }

Growing to this age, I realize, is kind of like feeling your voice deepen. It's still your voice, but it has more substance, and it sounds like it knows its own origins. As my voice grows, I look forward to the roles I will play—and to celebrating the women I'll bring to life on the screen. Even more important, I look forward to getting to know the people I'll meet on those journeys.

In 2002, more women will turn 50 than in any previous year. The force of that collective power fulfills and inspires me. It's thrilling to know that everywhere in the world, women are working, thinking, daring, creating, making change. I don't know if our mothers ever felt this way about their counterparts—but I have the feeling that our daughters will.

So welcome to the world of 50! This is a book about taking risks, breaking boundaries, becoming. I salute the women in these pages with pride. They have paved the way for us while making it possible for our children to smile as they embrace the unknown.

GROWING TO THIS age IS KIND OF LIKE FEELING YOUR VOICE DEEPEN. IT'S STILL YOUR VOICE, BUT IT HAS more SUBSTANCE.

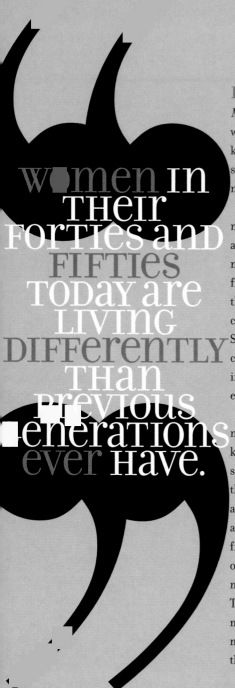

Women in their forties and fifties today are living differently than previous generations ever have.

BY MYRNA BLYTH, EDITOR-IN-CHIEF, *more* magazine

MORE magazine is delighted to present a book that celebrates fifty extraordinary women who are nearing 50, turning 50, or making the most of their fifties. *MORE*, as I hope you know, is the only magazine that focuses entirely on the lifestyle of women between forty and sixty. In every issue, we cover successful, charismatic women who, in today's world, have more opportunities for self-fulfillment and self-satisfaction than ever before.

MORE was launched a little more than three years ago. It began because, as an avid magazine reader, I felt left out. There were so many publications for the young—newsstands are filled with them—but magazines tend to ignore women once they hit forty. There were no magazines that showed fashion on models who are near my age or the age of most of my friends. That just didn't seem right. It also bothered me that I could never find articles about the subjects those same friends and I often talked about, such as dealing with young adult children or aging parents. I also realized that many women at midlife have other concerns. Some long to have or to adopt a child. Others crave a change in direction, wanting a new career or an entirely different way of life. But there was no publication that had much information, or much empathy, for us.

As a long-time magazine editor, I knew I had to do something to rectify this. So, together with { **INTROD** an extremely talented and dedicated team, I developed and launched *MORE*. Some facts about the magazine: Since its first issue, it has enjoyed considerable success, increasing its frequency and almost doubling its circulation within the first couple of years. Every model on our pages is over forty. Every issue combines beauty, fashion, health, relationship, travel, money, and lifestyle features. Why did we name it *MORE*? I know I have to explain that one. To be absolutely honest, it was the name we disliked the least when we were developing the magazine. But then, when a reporter interviewed me during the magazine's launch, I found myself saying, "Women over forty used to expect less, now they want more." She said, "So that's why you named it *MORE*." "Of course," I replied gratefully.

As it turns out, *MORE* is exactly the right name for the magazine—and for the generation we write about. While working on the launch, I met Dr. Martha Farnsworth Riche, a leading demographer and former director of the U.S. Census Bureau. Dr. Riche has a theory about aging that I think is exactly right. We all know that women today live about twenty years longer than women did in the past. But Dr. Riche believes we haven't tacked those years onto the end of our life. We've added them in the middle, stretching our most productive, most vital, most enjoyable years. Women in their forties and fifties today are living differently than previous generations ever have. They have more options and opportunities. They can be more self-indulgent or more experimental, more caring or more outspoken. They can look and feel their best. The women in this book confirm this wonderful new reality.

Another important fact: Women today are valued for their experience. That has never happened before. For century after century, women were valued only for innocence, for fertility, for youthful beauty—all qualities related to the lack of experience. But for the generation now in midlife, women, like men, are valued for the experience that comes with age—experience that leads to further accomplishment. It is an extraordinary change, and one that benefits every woman.

The baby boom generation is the largest segment of our population. More women will turn 50 in 2002 than ever before—and over the next five years, women in unprecedented numbers will be celebrating this important birthday. Once, turning 50 was an event that women tended to ignore or deny. Not any more.

uction

Of course, I know that many women still feel the Big Five-O is a milestone. And at *MORE*, readers often write to tell us how they are celebrating their special day. This birthday has always been a time to look back. But now, women know it is also a time to celebrate and to look ahead. We want this book to be part of that celebration.

The 50 women in these pages are between the ages of 47 and 56. All have been interviewed by *MORE* magazine. You will learn from them, and you will be entertained and inspired by them; I know I am. Their stories are told in a variety of ways. Some are profiled, while others speak to the reader either directly or through a question-and-answer format. Many are well known, and all are interesting because they have marvelous life stories—stories only women of this phenomenal generation could tell. Share some time with them and I think you'll agree that women's lives today are like those chocolate sandwich cookies. Yes, the good stuff is in the middle.

once, turning 50 was an event that women tended to ignore or deny. Not any more.

Bree

Occupation:
Reporter, Producer
Born:
February 26, 1953

Walker

AGAINST THE ODDS ▷ For more than two decades, Emmy winner Bree Walker was one of Southern California's most celebrated television news reporters. During that time, she also became an outspoken advocate for people with disabilities and was appointed by the Presidents George H. Bush and Bill Clinton to sit on the Committee on Employment of the Handicapped. Walker was born with ectrodactyly, a rare genetic condition that her two children, who are 13 and 10, have inherited, which results in fused fingers, small palms, and short or missing thumbs. Recently she left television news to form her own production company.

question: During your second pregnancy, you were criticized on a "shock" radio show for the decision to have another child who might inherit your disability. How did that affect you?

answer: It was a devastating time for me. It's not that the subject shouldn't be open to discussion—but my husband and I weren't informed of the show until it had aired. Our opinions and those of other disability-rights advocates weren't heard. There was this assumption my children would be dependent on tax dollars to support them, which is absolutely ridiculous. Despite my disability, I've been working since I was 16. I ultimately began to feel like I wanted to set more meaningful goals for myself.

question: What did those goals turn out to be?

answer: I began to refocus my priorities. It's been so easy for us boomers to define ourselves by our successes and accomplishments instead of what we've become. I think we, the peace and love generation, haven't done such a good job raising our kids. While our heads were turned—focused on our careers—we let violence creep into our society. We're now harvesting the crop: children raised on video games, television shows, and movies that use violence as a coping mechanism.

question: Are you raising your children differently than you were, in regard to their disabilities?

answer: My parents taught me it was my job to make people feel comfortable; that I should always be the one to extend my hand. Growing up, it was an enormous responsibility. (My mother suffered from ectrodactyly, but doctors did not know what to call it back then; they thought it was rheumatoid arthritis.) I tell my children that they have every right to be on this earth and to expect tolerance. I won't say there isn't a problem with bullies. But usually, when I ask how I can help them, they tend to want to deal with it themselves by leaving the situation alone. Hopefully, I've taught my children to love themselves and to know that diversity is what makes the planet interesting and valuable.

> { "I tell my children that they have every right to be on this earth and to expect tolerance." }

Jeanne

moutoussamy-ashe

Occupation:
Photographer
Born:
July 9, 1951

THE TRUE PICTURE ▷ It has been said that Jeanne Moutoussamy-Ashe's camera

is an extension of both her goals and her persona. A celebrated fine arts photographer, she has devoted much of her life to civic causes in health, arts education, and urban issues. Her work has appeared in numerous publications, including *Life*, *Sports Illustrated*, and the *New York Times*, and has been shown in solo and group exhibits around the world. She is the author of *Daufuskie Island: A Photographic Essay*, which explores the lives of the descendants of slaves, and *Viewfinders*, an anthology of early black women photographers. Her children's book, *Daddy and Me*, affectionately chronicles the final days of her late husband, tennis legend and social activist Arthur Ashe. (Ashe, who died in 1993 of AIDS-related pneumonia, contracted AIDS from a tainted blood transfusion received during heart surgery.) The couple's daughter, Camera, is 15.

"I guess the most striking thing about turning 50 is that I'm still here. When I was tested for AIDS and found healthy, that was a miracle. I had already lost my oldest brother to a heart attack when he was 39; Arthur was 49. I have accepted death as an event, one that is as much a part of life as birth. You just hope when it arrives you're ready, and that you can leave behind good works. I know Arthur could say that, and I need to be able to say that as well.

{ "I realize now that though I was always independent, I was also the copilot." }

"I realize now that though I was always independent, I was also the copilot—or at least I was for 17 years with Arthur. Now I am not just independent; I'm also self-reliant. I had thought about becoming a copilot again, but realize I don't have to do that. It's not what I need to help me grow.

"The way I look at life is also reflected in my more recent photographs. My earlier work mostly reflected my attempt to impose my sense of order on chaos. Today, I am much more centered and focused on quiet themes, such as botanicals. Before, I used to shoot rolls and rolls of film and turn them over to a processor. Now, I develop my own work, spending hours in the darkroom. It's my way of saying that it takes going into the darkness to come to the light.

"Shortly after turning 50, I mounted a show, published a book about the exhibit, and set up a website. It was quite an undertaking for me, but I planned it that way. The name of the show was *Transitions*, because I was and am truly a person in transition.

"Now, in the third phase of my life, whatever else happens is icing on the cake. I've had a great education, I've been blessed with a skill, I've had a partner for 17 years, and I am a mother. What I am left with is my own person, still in development. I am truly pleased with where I am going."

meryl

streep

Occupation:
Actress
Born:
June 22, 1949

{Family Matters} For her fiftieth birthday, Meryl Streep didn't want anything at all. Nothing tangible, that is. "All my friends wanted big, elaborate parties," she says. "All I wanted was more time. And nobody could give that to me as a present, all wrapped up with a ribbon." For Streep, who has been called America's greatest living actress, kicking back has always been important—especially with her family, her priority throughout an extraordinary career. Nominated 12 times for an Academy Award, she has received two Oscars, for 1979's *Kramer vs. Kramer* and 1982's *Sophie's Choice.* Then there

are the Golden Globes—14 nominations, three awards—and an Emmy Award for the 1978 television miniseries *Holocaust.* While many actresses of Streep's skill have branched out into directing, "I haven't chosen to because of the time commitment," she says. "With a director, it doesn't stop at 6 p.m. I would have to deal with it on family time, on the kids' time, on Don's time."

Don is sculptor Donald Gummer, Streep's husband of 24 years and father of her four children—three daughters and a son, ranging in age from 10 to 22. When choosing which role to play next, the actress always keeps her family in mind, in terms not only of time but also of location and content. "It's different for every film, but location, location, location is almost always the first or second priority," she says. "We've sort of made a pact in the family that I would never be away more than two weeks. And I think, too, 'Does the film give anything? Or does it rape the world, strip-mine the soul of the culture?'"

Meticulous about preparing for a role—for 1999's *Music of the Heart,* she studied and played the violin six hours a day for four months—she has said that the mysterious part of the psyche she calls upon to portray a character borders on the sacred.

Streep studied opera as a young girl and later earned degrees from Vassar College and the Yale School of Drama. She's also a veteran of New York's prestigious Public Theater. (She reportedly turned down the opportunity to head it after the death of founder Joseph Papp.) A serious woman with a private life and a public conscience, she has shunned the Hollywood lifestyle, instead living quietly in the Connecticut countryside. "We don't go anywhere, or do anything," she says. "We're sort of not in that world, whatever that world is—mostly because we don't enjoy it very much. I don't like going to openings. And I don't love seeing my picture all over everything."

What she has been public about is Mothers and Others, a consumer-interest group she and some of her neighbors have formed to explore environmental issues primarily affecting the younger generation. "I started with twenty of my friends, and now we have about 30,000 members subscribing to our newsletter, *The Green Guide,* which talks about all sorts of preventative and consumer-interest issues that are important to parents," she says.

The notion of becoming a part of the older generation does not seem to faze Streep. Though she has admitted that menopause has affected her ability to memorize lines, she once told a television interviewer that being older actually makes it easier to access certain emotions, because "you've been through the wringer more."

And what will happen to Streep's career once all the children are grown? She would like to continue exploring her roots, the theater. "I dream of it all the time," she says. "I'd like to do more Chekhov. I really love Chekhov—he's such a humanist."

ALL I wanted was more time. AND NOBODY COULD GIVE THAT TO me as a present, aLL wrapped up with a ribbon.

JUDY

Occupation:
Education Fundraiser
Born:
May 9, 1948

GEHrKE

aT FULL THROTTLE ▷ In 1973, Judy Gehrke was in the top 5 percent of her Harvard Business School class. Brilliant, funny, and outspoken, she was the perfect candidate to become a CEO—or, perhaps, to marry one. She did neither. Instead, she chose a vocation that "does a lot of good for a lot of people," and she married a man who arranges his work schedule around his hobby: playing chess. Gehrke, 54, and her husband of 24 years have one teenage son.

"I love my fifties, because I can experience full throttle the course my life has taken and be totally comfortable with the decisions that led me here," says Gehrke. "I have a great job that I look forward to every day." As executive director of Greenflea, Inc., Gehrke helps to raise money for New York City public schools.

The daughter of a Milwaukee brewery worker, Gehrke graduated from Northwestern University with a degree in Russian literature. She received a master's degree in design from Pratt Institute before getting her M.B.A. at Harvard. Back then, women in business school were an anomaly. "In a class of 800, there were only 38 of us," she says. "Prior to that, women were just something business school graduates married." Business degree in hand, Gehrke wasn't ready for wifehood. She began the corporate grind soon after graduation. After a decade of changing jobs, moving to larger companies for bigger salaries and traveling extensively, she began to feel the corporate ladder never rose above a 45-degree angle. One day she realized that she was doing what was expected of her, not what she really wanted to do.

{ "I like the person I see in the mirror every morning. She smiles at me." }

Gehrke likes the flexibility of the job she now holds. "I basically set my own hours," she explains. She prides herself on the fact that her job raises money for education, which "should be a national priority," she says. "Greenflea was a mostly volunteer organization when I took over 10 years ago," she notes. Under her direction the organization's $600,000 annual budget has nearly doubled to $1 million.

When Gehrke reflects on her own success, she points to an inner peace: "I do all right financially; my family takes at least one exciting vacation a year, and we've managed to save for our son's college. I like the person I see in the mirror every morning. She smiles at me."

Gehrke also likes being married to "my biggest fan, my greatest supporter, my best friend." Luis Rodriguez, who owns a paint contracting firm, has opened many doors for his wife: When they first met, he was the doorman in her New York City apartment building.

Occupation:
Fashion Designer
Born:
May 9, 1947

JOSIE

natori

DESIGNING WOMAN ▷ Josie Natori, noted fashion designer and CEO of Natori Company, is a classically trained pianist who was a solo performer with the Manila Philharmonic Orchestra at age 9. A graduate of Manhattanville College with a degree in economics, she has that rare combination of creative genius and business acumen. In her early twenties, she became the first woman vice president in investment banking for Merrill Lynch. At 29, she left her six-figure salary to start a fashion business—something she knew absolutely nothing about—and became the first to turn innerwear into outerwear, designing elegant lingerie for day. She is married to Japanese businessman Ken Natori, who left Wall Street to become her business partner. They have one son, Kenneth Jr., 26, who is a journalist.

question: What were your thoughts when you turned 50?

answer: At 50, I had more energy than three 20-year-olds. For my birthday, I rented out Carnegie Hall and gave a piano concert for twenty-eight hundred people. In preparation, I practiced for three years. To date, nothing in my life has been as exhilarating. But then, who knows? Maybe at 60 I'll top myself.

question: Why do you think you were so successful in a business at which you had no experience?

answer: I was willing to take risks and listen.

{ "It's important to keep in shape, to look good, because it follows naturally that you will feel good." }

Very few people really listen today. I didn't know anything about fashion, only what I liked. But I knew I had good taste and a sense of style. People always commented on what I wore, so I was confident in that area. I trusted my instincts and knew I had a good idea, and my timing was right. Most of all, I listened to what the buyers said they wanted.

question: Some women seem to think that when they get older, they can't be as stylish anymore. What do you think?

answer: My older female relatives were wonderful, but they all let their waistlines go once they reached middle age. Now, I'm not so sure what middle age is, but I do know that it's important to keep in shape, to look good, because it follows naturally that you will feel good. There's no reason to feel boundaries in regard to what we can accomplish. And that includes continuing with our own sense of style—whatever that may be, no matter what our age.

question: What is your definition of success?

answer: When you are able to make a difference in other people's lives. I think successful people have an obligation to give back.

ann

Occupation:
Explorer
Born:
September 29, 1955

Bancroft

{Dream Trekker} At 3, Ann Bancroft was skiing; at 8, she was leading cousins and neighborhood kids through expeditions on her parents' farm. By the time she was a preteen, she was canoeing wild rivers with her father. The experiences all would prove to be good training for Bancroft, a former schoolteacher who

"Fuel the mind with passion, and you can accomplish almost anything within reason."

recently became, along with her Norwegian friend Liv Arnesen, the first women to cross the continent of Antarctica on foot. (Arnesen earlier had been the first woman to ski alone to the South Pole.) Prior to the 1,717-mile, 94-day trek, Bancroft had notched another milestone, as the first woman to dogsled from the Northwest Territories of Canada to the North Pole. She and Arnesen met in 1998, when they discovered that they both had dreamed of an Antarctic crossing since childhood.

Bancroft, 46, says that the greatest training she received for her groundbreaking explorations was learning to cope with a childhood learning disability. "I was dyslexic during an era when nobody really knew what the condition was," she says. "They knew I was smart, but my grades didn't match." Early on, she discovered that "if I put one foot in front of the other, stuck with it, and honed my skills for a sense of purpose, I could get where I wanted to go."

Her powers of concentration enabled her to graduate from the University of Oregon. Soon afterward, she began a career teaching physical education and special education at an elementary school in Minneapolis, where she also coached a number of girls' sports teams. She also became an instructor for Wilderness Inquiry, which helps both disabled and able-bodied people enjoy the wilderness.

"I love being outdoors and I thrive on thermal challenges," Bancroft notes, adding that skiing across Antarctica in early 2001 presented a much greater mental challenge than a physical one. "The mind tells the body it is tired, but the body can do amazing things if you feed it correctly and treat it right. Fuel the mind with passion—and I have it for this kind of thing—and you can accomplish almost anything within reason."

Bancroft's latest expedition is Bancroft Arnesen Explore, a company that helps people, especially women, achieve their dreams through expedition funding and sponsorships. In May 2001, the organization helped sponsor 16 teen girls on an expedition to climb the 20,413-foot Nevado Chinchey mountain in the Peruvian Andes.

 Is so much activity daunting as she faces her fiftieth birthday? "Fifty is nothing more than a year that falls into a five-year plan," she says. "I'm in my late forties and still pursuing dreams. I never thought I'd be running a company and figuring out budgets.... Talk about exploring new territory!"

Any words for the wise? "No matter what your age, you have to do what turns you on," Bancroft notes. "Never let others decide what's important to you. People meet Liv and me and are surprised by our ages. They think, 'Hey, maybe there's hope for me.'"

JACLYN

TOUCHED BY an anGEL ▷ Long before Jaclyn Smith became famous as Kelly Garrett, one of Charlie's Angels in the Seventies TV series, she wanted to be a dancer. When she moved to New York to pursue that dream, she was sought after for modeling and acting jobs instead. After her role as an Angel ended in 1981, she continued to perform on the small screen, winning acclaim for her work in miniseries like *Rage of Angels* and *Jacqueline Bouvier Kennedy*. Today, the soft-spoken Smith continues acting and oversees her successful Kmart signature collection of women's casual clothes. Her focus, however, remains her family: children Gaston, 20, and Spencer Margaret, 16, and her husband, Bradley Allen, a pediatric heart surgeon who practices in Chicago and commutes weekly to the couple's home in Los Angeles.

question: As you've gotten older, have the job offers become fewer?

answer: I'm working less, but by choice. Last year, I turned down five movies and the chance to do *The Graduate* in London. I really wanted that role, but it would've meant being away from home for five months. With a teenager just learning to drive, it wasn't a good idea. Besides, I want to be with my children. I enjoy them so much, and my time at home with them is so fleeting.

question: *The Graduate*—now there's a sexy role for older women. What makes a woman sexy in midlife?

answer: Being comfortable in your own skin— and I don't mean nudity. It's being free: allowing your personality to emerge. But it's so subjective. With lighting and makeup, anyone can look sexy; then when you meet them in person, they can be cold. Sometimes sexiness is in the eye of the beholder.

{ What makes a woman "Being sexy in midlife? comfortable in your own skin." }

question: Did you dread turning 50?

answer: Until a couple years ago, I felt like a kid. I wasn't aware of any particular age. But then I started noticing strollers in the park and realized I didn't have babies anymore—that part of my life was over. I also began to see people I love growing older. Recently, it's been more of a recognition that certain moments will never be again, especially with my children.

question: Do you worry about the future?

answer: I have a wonderful life. If the acting roles dry up, it doesn't matter; I'll always be busy. I've learned to be more assertive as I've gotten older and have applied this to my role as a businesswoman with my Kmart line. I have my children, a wonderful husband—and who knows, sometimes I think about adopting a child. We'll see.

Occupation:
Actress
Born:
October 26, 1947

SMITH

a new recipe ▷

Ask celebrity chef Sara Moulton for her recipe for turning 50 and she'll refer you to Mrs. Ramsey, a character in Virginia Woolf's *To the Lighthouse*. The book, she says, was a landmark in her life as a budding feminist. "Although I admired her in many ways, Mrs. Ramsey was too self-sacrificing; she seemed to have no life of her own," Moulton explains. "On turning 50, I am resolving to resist my own tendency to act like Mrs. Ramsey. Sometimes I'm so busy taking care of business, I miss being there. I'm going to try to focus on slowing down and appreciating my family and myself."

That goal may not be easy to achieve: Moulton is chef du jour of three pressure cooker jobs—executive chef of *Gourmet* magazine, food editor of ABC-TV's *Good Morning America*, and star of the Food Network's *Cooking Live*. Stirring into the mix a hands-on role as mom to Ruthie, 15, and Sam, 11, Moulton says that, at this stage, she has learned at least one crucial ingredient for making life easier and expanding family time. "Leftovers are key," she says, with a laugh.

Moulton can't remember a time when she wasn't fascinated with food. As a child, she baked bread and cookies with her grandmother, then moved on to more exotic fare with her mother's help. On weekends at her family's country house, everyone cooked, making ample use of fresh herbs from the backyard garden.

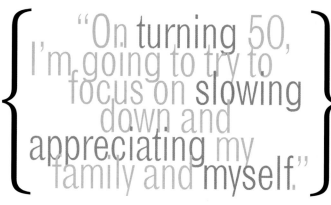

"On turning 50, I'm going to try to focus on slowing down and appreciating my family and myself."

While majoring in the history of ideas at the University of Michigan, Moulton never strayed far from a kitchen. She cooked for a professor's family, flipped burgers, and waitressed. At her mother's suggestion, she applied to the prestigious Culinary Institute of America in Hyde Park, New York. After graduation, the young chef studied and worked in France.

But Moulton learned soon enough that while women might rule in home kitchens, in professional settings it was men who wore the toques. "In restaurants, it's about men, power, and control," she declares. To form an "old girls' network," Moulton cofounded the New York Women's Culinary Alliance, a group that supports women in their bid for equal pay and opportunity. "It's all a matter of taking the heat and staying in the kitchen," she explains wryly.

This year, as Moulton and her husband of 21 years, music consultant Bill Adler, both turn 50, Moulton will have another important milestone to celebrate, when her first book, *Sara Moulton Cooks at Home*, arrives in bookstores. So, what's she cooking up to celebrate? "This is definitely a cake that should be loaded with calories," she laughs. "At 50, you need to splurge!"

sara

Occupation:
TV & Magazine Chef
Born:
February 19, 1952

moulton

Diane

Keaton

Occupation:
Actress, Director
Born:
January 5, 1946

{Baby Boom} "I want to keep expressing myself until I'm finished—until I'm not alive," says Diane Keaton of her creative endeavors, which include photography, acting, directing—and compiling eclectic designs from magazines in scrapbooks. Of the latter activity, Keaton says, "It's a way of life, even if I don't have an audience."

At 56, Keaton actually has two audiences—her adoring public and, of late, her two children. The self-effacing actress, whom many will always associate with her Academy Award-winning role in 1977's *Annie Hall*, became a single mom at age 50, when she adopted daughter Dexter, now 6. In February 2001, she brought home a baby boy named Duke.

"The turning point was when my dad got sick," Keaton says. "There was just no way I could procrastinate anymore. I said to myself, 'Are you going to start a family, or aren't you?'"

As a result of her decision, the never-married Keaton got rid of her exquisitely constructed house in the Hollywood Hills and moved into a cluttered home in Beverly Hills that is scattered with baby toys. Friends insist she's much happier.

"It's astonishing; it's another world," she says, confiding that despite having paid help, "the work of raising kids gives me a heightened appreciation of the women's movement." Friends also say raising children has made her less scattered.

"I have my priorities in order," she says. "There's a separation between work and my personal life. My work, which I love, is not the necessary component it once was. I don't have time to think about it that way."

Time is something Keaton plans never again to waste. "I wish I'd come to my senses sooner, that I'd been more with-it in my early thirties," she confesses. "I wish I'd just gotten over a lot of relationships that I held onto forever." Keaton, who in the Seventies was Woody Allen's lover and muse, also had intense relationships with Warren Beatty and Al Pacino. Today she says that romance is "probably out of the picture. I'm not a big social person."

All the same, Keaton doesn't feel she's missing anything socially or professionally—even though she knows that "when actors get older, they are less valuable in marketing terms." In light of this, she was surprised and delighted at the overwhelming success of *The First Wives Club*, the 1996 movie she starred in with Goldie Hawn and Bette Midler about the trials and tribulations of three middle-aged women. "It saved my life," she laughs.

OBSTACLES keep coming at you. You just

Directing, Keaton says, was the next challenge. "It's what I want to do," she says. "Obstacles keep coming at you. You just have to keep going through them—because it's worth it to do something in your life, as opposed to just fantasizing about doing something."

As for the next decade? "In 10 years, I just hope I'm really healthy, mentally and physically, so I can be vital in raising my kids," she declares. "That's my first and foremost thought. I also hope to continue taking opportunities that interest me, so I can remain vibrant and alive— and give my children a good life."

have to keep going through them. ”

PAULA

MADISON

BREAKING BARRIERS ▷ As president and general manager of KNBC-TV in Los Angeles, Paula Madison is the first African-American woman to hold those titles in a top-five television market. Prior to that, she was vice president and news director at New York City's WNBC-TV, the first African-American woman in either role in the nation's number one news market. Madison and her husband live in Los Angeles and Westchester County, New York. They have one daughter, Imani, who is a second-year medical student.

question: What was it like growing up in Harlem a half century ago?

answer: We were really poor; I didn't know how poor because I had nothing to compare it with. But amidst the poverty, there were also people doing the best they could to raise their children. My parents were separated, and we were on welfare, but the environment was rich for building character. We couldn't afford a Christmas tree, so on December 24, we'd pick up what was left on the street. I grew up with scraggly Christmas trees trimmed with homemade ornaments that we treasured—and we were happy.

question: How did you escape poverty yourself?

answer: By making a vow to have it end with my generation. My parents instilled in us the importance of education. I made good grades, went to Vassar on a scholarship, worked hard at what I did, and had mentors. Sometimes the mentors were female, sometimes people of color—but very often they were white males. People often ask, "What's it like to be 'the first'?" I always answer that somewhere along the line, we have to recognize that there are people willing to look beyond their own reflections in the mirror so that they can embrace and support diversity. That is how we get where we are.

question: So, when you celebrate 50, will it be a truly happy birthday?

answer: I've never had a birthday that depressed me. Turning 50 is certainly no reason to start. There was one birthday that coincidentally fell on my annual pajama party.

question: You still have pajama parties?

answer: Every year, I get together with about 15 women friends—teachers, lawyers, judges, doctors—who are all in their late thirties to sixties. We stay up all night dancing to The Dells, James Brown, Ike and Tina Turner—it's often Motown revisited! We talk about menopause, children, husbands, work, money, fashion, our parents getting old. And we eat. We live for these get-togethers and we'll be doing them when we're 80.

{ "Every year I get together with about 15 women friends. We stay up all night dancing." }

SANDWICH TIME ▷ With daughter Bonney going off to college, Ruth Widmann was looking forward to some downtime: travel, perhaps, and hobbies. However, shortly after Widmann turned 50, her mother, suffering from Alzheimer's, came to live with her. Then Bonney decided to move back home, to help out and attend a local college. Widmann, pastor of Valhalla United Methodist Church in Westchester County, New York, is divorced.

"I turned 50 in Germany, hosting a church tour to the Passion Play in Obergammergau. The trip was a present to myself, as well as my high school graduation gift to my daughter. I've been a single mom since Bonney was 3. We used to do a lot together and were always close.

"Now, with my mother in the house, the dynamic of our relationship has changed. Meals are the only time we really have together, and they are especially difficult. I try to talk with Bonney, but mother always interrupts. I want to respect my mother and include her, but the focus always shifts away from Bonney and ends up on her.

"My daughter is a wonderful, compassionate young woman, and I know this is hard on her. We made the decision together about my mother living here. When my father died, I promised him I'd take care of her. When her memory got really bad, I just couldn't put her in a nursing home. I felt she wouldn't get the compassionate care she needed.

"My mother is in day care during the week. At night Bonney studies and, after dinner, I work until at least 10, so we have an aide. On Saturdays, I'm with my mother all day, and on Sundays, when I'm in church, Bonney watches her. If you looked at my schedule on paper, you'd say it's not doable. Even I wonder how it's possible. One thing this process has taught me is to take one day at a time.

"Ordinarily I'm easygoing, but there are times I feel stressed. I gain strength in quiet, but finding that time is another story. I don't cry like I used to. It's still sad because my mother's at the point where she knows she doesn't know things. Sometimes, she asks if she'll get better. I don't want to take away her hope, so I tell her scientists are working on it.

"I know this is a phase. The time will come when my mother will die and Bonney will leave. I accept that. I see this as an opportunity to grow into the person I was meant to be, to learn to be more compassionate and helpful. Even in the most difficult times, I'm glad I have this time to do what I'm doing—caring for my mother as she cared for me."

{ "I'm glad I have this time to do what I'm doing— caring for my mother as she cared for me." }

ruth

Occupation: Methodist Pastor
Born: August 16, 1950

widmann

reBa

Occupation:
Musician, Actress
Born:
March 28, 1955

mcentire

{Raising Her Voice} "I love my forties better than my thirties—and I'm looking forward to my fifties," says Reba McEntire. A woman whose career over the past two decades has grown and expanded with each passing year, the energetic redhead is currently the country's all-time top-selling female recording artist. But, she says, it was not her singing voice alone that helped sell more than 46 million CDs. "It was also my inner voice—the one that told me to take charge," she laughs. These two voices have proven to be a potent combination, allowing McEntire to become one of the first women

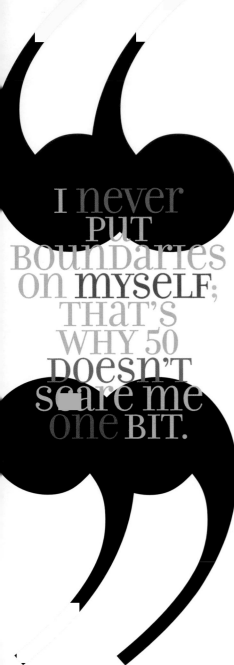

I never put boundaries on myself; that's why 50 doesn't scare me one bit.

in Nashville to manage her own career at a time and in a place where outspoken women weren't usually heard.

McEntire was still in college at Southeastern Oklahoma State University when she was discovered, belting out "The Star Spangled Banner" at a rodeo in 1974. Within a year she had a record deal. "In my twenties, the only thing I knew for a fact was that I could sing," she says. As she matured she learned a lot about herself, some of it, she confesses, "the hard way."

Married in 1976 at age 21 to a three-time international-rodeo steer-wrestling champ, she was happy "singing, ranching, and rodeoing" and letting others make her career decisions. But by the mid-Eighties, she was deciding what songs she would sing and which cuts would appear on albums. "I felt there had to be a better way of doing things for my career and for me," she says. "It was just a gut feeling I had, and I took it to mean that God was telling me what to do." The result was *My Kind of Country*, her breakthrough album. Over the next four years—1984 through 1987—she received four Female Vocalist of the Year awards from the Country Music Association.

McEntire, of course, was delighted by her success. But her husband, 10 years her senior, urged her to retire so they could spend more time together. While his career was winding down, hers was just starting, and it soon became clear that their lives were going in different directions. So when the limelight beckoned, McEntire spoke up once again. In 1987, on the couple's eleventh wedding anniversary, she filed for divorce and went on to her next show.

She wouldn't stay single for long. By June 1989, she was married again, this time to Narvel Blackstock, her road manager. Together they have built both a family—their son, Shelby, is 11—and an entertainment empire. "When I realized I was thinking of my career more than anyone else was, that's when I decided to form my own company," she explains.

McEntire's business conglomerate includes her own management, booking, music publishing, and film production companies. She is that rare person who possesses both creative talent and good business instincts. "I've been around hardworking people all my life," she says. "I watched my daddy handle his cattle and deal with bankers. He was a world champion cowboy, a rancher, and a businessman."

In the past 25 years, McEntire has recorded 27 albums, won a Grammy, appeared in several movies, and written two books. The year 2001 brought two high-profile projects that tested the range of her talents: a much-applauded starring role in Broadway's *Annie Get Your Gun* and the lead in *Reba*, a sitcom that premiered on the WB network. "I never put boundaries on myself," says McEntire. "I've always been willing to take chances, since I'm curious and I love a good challenge. That's why 50 doesn't scare me one bit. Each birthday, I thank God that I'm still doing what I love to do."

50/50:

Reba
McEntire

SECOND ACT ▷ Comedy can be serious business for Wendy Wasserstein. Celebrated for her dramatic explorations of boomer women torn between career ambition and personal fulfillment, the acclaimed playwright has brought humor and pathos to a variety of everyday dilemmas. Although her characters don't always reflect her persona, their conflicts are close to her heart. In 1989, the Yale graduate—who's also penned musicals and a children's book—won both a Pulitzer and a Tony for her fourth play, *The Heidi Chronicles*. She was 38. As the curtain rises more than a decade later, she finds herself embracing a new challenge: motherhood.

question: Was 50 a benchmark for you?

answer: No, but I didn't want it to be. I really didn't think about being 50. I may have had a small cocktail party in my home to celebrate, but I had just come through a decade of looking at death and then life. It doesn't get any more dramatic than that. I lost my sister to breast cancer. She was an extraordinary person. We were very close, and I still miss her enormously. Not long after that, at 48, I had a daughter.

question: Was your sister's death the reason you wanted a child?

answer: I had tried throughout my forties to get pregnant, but nothing happened. I gave up for a while during my sister's illness, but then started trying again. On September 12, 1999, Lucy Jane was born. She's changed my life completely.

question: How so?

answer: Being a mother has given my life a depth of responsibility I never had before—I am just so much happier. Now, I believe in miracles, since she's truly a miracle. Because

{ "Being a mother has given my life a depth of responsibility I never had before—I am just so much happier." }

I was older when I gave birth, I have to be more mindful of my health; I have to think not only about my future, but also about hers and who will take care of her. It's quite a commitment.

question: What do you do differently now from when you were in your thirties?

answer: I no longer get in bed with a box of pizza and cry because a man didn't call. I just don't have the time anymore.

question: Any regrets?

answer: I'm never going to be 28 and getting married. I'm never going to have spent 30 years of my life with somebody. So I won't know commitment on that level, but I probably also won't know jealousy and envy and hatred on that level either.

wendy

Occupation:
Playwright
Born:
October 18, 1950

wasserstein

sandy

peterson

HEALING OLD WOUNDS ▷ In 1968, Army recruiters paid a visit to St. Mary's Hospital in Rochester, New York, offering to pay the final year of nursing school for those willing to serve in Vietnam. Twenty-year-old Sandy Peterson signed on. After graduation and basic training, she was sent to the 18th Surgical Hospital in Quang Tri, not far from the DMZ. She served 15 months. Never married, Peterson lives in Stockton, California, with her adopted son, 14, and continues her nursing career as manager of Dameron Hospital's endoscopy department.

"Except for the AARP notice that came in the mail, I paid no attention to my fiftieth birthday. I don't think about age, because I don't sweat the small stuff. Even the most horrendous day is a piece of cake compared to any day I spent in Vietnam.

"When I arrived there in April 1970, I awoke to the sound of bombs that kept getting closer and closer. I thought, 'What have I done to myself?' Later, when I walked into the officers' club, there was a standing ovation. I thought Bob Hope had arrived, but they were actually saluting me and the other nurses because we'd volunteered to be there.

"Not long after that, a pilot I'd made friends with was brought in and died. I'd seen the war on the news, but this was real, and I was totally unprepared. I block out a lot, especially the times I sat at soldiers' bedsides so they wouldn't die alone. I'd hold their hand. They always talked about home.

{ "Even the most horrendous day is a piece of cake compared to any day I spent in Vietnam." }

"The Vietcong were always shelling our airfield. I think the hospital was spared because we cared for Vietcong children, ones who had been given grenades to throw at our GIs but had blown up themselves instead.

"Then when I got home, there was the anger. I got off the plane, and protesters spit on my uniform. My dad had been in World War II, and he was the only one who understood a little of what I'd been through.

"For years, I had horrible dreams. During the day, anything—even a smell—could set off a whole set of fears. I thought it was just me. That began to change in the mid-Eighties, when I connected with some Vietnam vets raising money for a memorial in Sacramento. It became my group therapy. Nurses heal everybody else; you never think of healing yourself.

"In 1987, I adopted a baby boy from India. I'd been exposed to Agent Orange and didn't want to risk having my own—a child who might be born and then just die. I sometimes take my son with me to veteran functions and try to explain things. He listens; I hope he understands."

AN ICON GROWS UP ▷ "I can't honestly tell you the greatest thing about being in my fifties—I've just now gotten here, and there's still so much left to do," says Twiggy, who rose to fame in the Sixties and Seventies as the coltish girl-woman who graced a thousand magazine covers. The "it girl" of a generation has played many roles in her life: model, television and theater star, wife and mother. These days, she's turned her interests to business, having recently launched a line of holistic skin care products based on aromatherapy. "People say I don't look my age," she says. "A lot has to do with using my own products, but a lot also has to do with my attitude. I still like taking risks. It keeps me passionate and I don't get bored."

That attitude served her well in 1966, when, along with the Beatles, the Rolling Stones, "mod" clothes, and miniskirts, she was at the forefront of the "British invasion" in America. Twiggy (born Leslie Hornby) was only 17 when she first came to the United States. Big-eyed, stick-legged, waiflike, and lovable, she was part icon and part myth, setting the standard by which we measured style.

In 1971, Twiggy had taken her first big risk, trading modeling for the silver screen as the star of Ken Russell's musical comedy *The Boy Friend*. A dozen years later, at 33, she was nominated for a Tony Award for her Broadway performance in *My One and Only*.

Between life's acts, Twiggy managed to marry, divorce, and marry again. She raised a daughter,

{ "I still like taking risks. It keeps me passionate and I don't get bored." }

Carly, and has a stepson, Ace, with Leigh Lawson, her husband of 13 years. She continues to appear on television in everything from sitcoms to chat shows; in the summer of 2001 she launched a series in Great Britain called *Take Time with Twiggy*. "I'd just like to keep on doing what I'm doing now," she says. "Especially having birthdays, since I adore presents! My fiftieth was particularly great, because my husband threw me a surprise party at my favorite restaurant."

The celebration, as it turned out, was bittersweet; it had been a difficult year. After four years in a nursing home, the actress's mother had died after a poignant struggle with dementia. "Though it had been difficult for her and for all of us when we first admitted her, in the end, I believe she was happy," she says. "The people who looked after her, I truly believe, are angels," she says.

Today, Twiggy is grateful for a life well lived. "I've got a lovely family," she says. "I think a lot of people get so muddled up in this business. It's lovely to be adored on stage or in film, but that's not life."

TWIGGY

Occupation:
Actress, Model
Born:
September 19, 1949

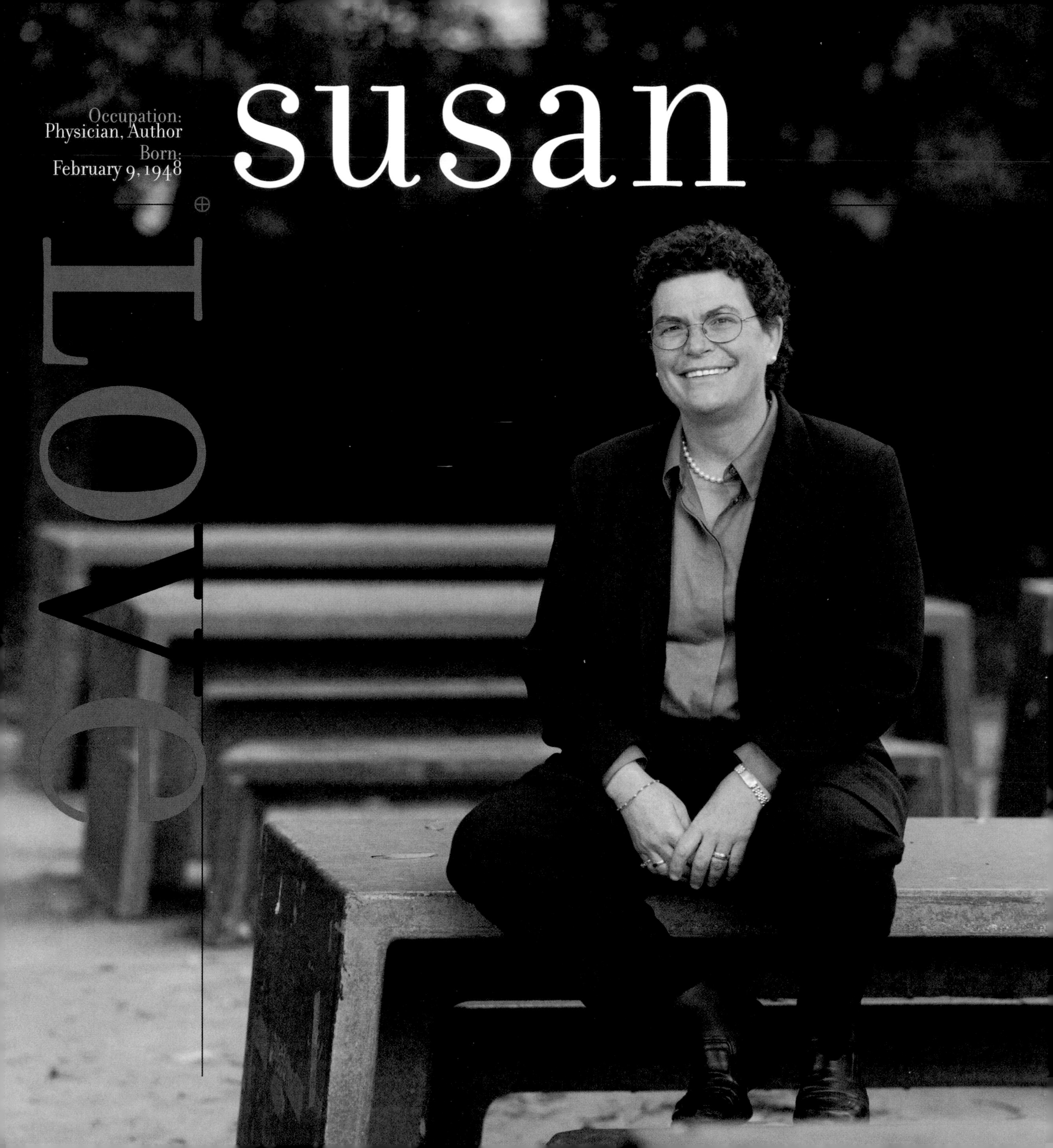

susan

Occupation:
Physician, Author
Born:
February 9, 1948

Love

{The Love Connection} Dr. Susan Love, cofounder of the National Breast Cancer Coalition, is an adjunct professor of surgery at UCLA and medical director of the Susan Love M.D. Breast Cancer Foundation. One of the best-known practitioners in her field, she's the author of *Dr. Susan Love's Breast Book*— a pioneering work widely acclaimed as a resource for women, especially those with breast cancer— and *Dr. Susan Love's Hormone Book*, which provides advice on menopause. She was appointed by President Clinton to the National Cancer Advisory Board.

question: Did you always want to be a doctor?

answer: When I was really little, I wanted to be a fireman. I liked the idea of the hat and the truck. Ultimately, I wanted to help people in some way. But in college, my adviser said I shouldn't go to med school because I'd be killing a boy—in other words, I'd be taking the place of a man who would otherwise end up in Vietnam. At that time, most med schools had quotas anyway: Only 5 percent of a class could be women, and they were filled by the time I applied. I ended up at Downstate Medical College in Brooklyn, New York, which was considered very liberal. It had a 10 percent quota.

question: Is it true you once joined a convent?

answer: I wasn't into drugs in the Sixties. So when others were rebelling, I thought the best way to upset my mother was to join a convent. I was a terrible nun—hanging out windows dressed in my habit, smoking cigarettes. I really think the convent was a way for me to avoid heterosexual sex.

question: When did you know you were gay?

answer: After I finished my residency, I decided it was time to get married. I ran a personal ad, and one guy responded to both me and to a friend of mine. I suddenly realized I was more interested in her than him. Soon afterward, I met my partner, Helen. We've been together 18 years. We wanted children, but she couldn't get pregnant. Being Irish Catholic, I got pregnant right away. Helen's first cousin is our daughter's father.

question: In terms of health care, what's the biggest lie women are being told today?

answer: That we all need hormone replacement therapy. Every woman's menopause is different—and, therefore, so are her needs. Menopause scares women because they can't control it. We have to realize it's a natural, inevitable process.

menopause scares women because they

question: What was your own experience with menopause?

answer: If there was a symptom, I had it. I'd go six months without a period, then bleed for months on end. I'd miss periods, have hot flashes, take estrogen, and start my periods again. I also had migraines. But it was all part of Mother Nature's plan. If it hadn't been so bad, I might never have written my book.

question: What's the best part of being 50?

answer: You can do just about anything you set your mind to—if, of course, you can remember to do it! Last year, I ran my first marathon. I exercised regularly and changed my diet. Living right is hard. My next mission: learning to play piano.

can't control it. we have to realize it's a natural, inevitable process.

Lynn Forester

Occupation:
CEO
Born:
July 2, 1954

TYCOON ▷ In 1990, after five years at Metromedia Telecommunications, 36-year-old Lynn Forester decided to be her own boss. Over the next five years, the Columbia-educated lawyer bought a small communications firm and sold it for a reported $25 million profit; soon afterwards, she founded another, which she also sold. That transaction netted her $10 million in cash and 5 percent of the purchasing company's stock, reportedly worth nearly $100 million. In 1997, Forester founded a third company—FirstMark Holdings, LLC—and today is CEO of FirstMark Communications Europe, which specializes in wireless technology. In 2000, the socialite and Democratic fundraiser married Sir Evelyn de Rothschild, the billionaire, then 69 years old, who heads the venerable Rothschild Bank in London. She has two teenage sons, Ben and Jake, from a previous marriage.

{ "What I didn't give up on was the possibility of having an interesting life." }

question: When you sold your first business, you made enough money that you'd never have to work again. Why start another company?

answer: I was 41, and actually planned to be a stay-at-home mom. I even fired the nanny. But a week later, I hired her back when I saw an opportunity in a new communications frontier and wanted to be a part of it.

question: With a London-based husband, a European-based business, and sons in New York, you must spend a lot of time in the air.

answer: Too much; every week or two I'm back and forth. Fortunately, I'm still able to see my boys a lot because of the arrangement I worked out with their father. But I'm not a soccer mom—and that's fine with my boys. It's the other mothers who begrudge me not always being there. My sons are proud of my accomplishments.

question: You're turning 50 soon. What are your thoughts?

answer: When I hear 50, I think of my mother—certainly not me! I don't think in terms of age. After all, you're talking to someone who recently married a vibrant, youthful 69-year-old man.

question: Did you think you'd remarry?

answer: When one of my businesses didn't go in the direction I planned, I looked at the disappointment as an opportunity. My divorce, however, was a troubling failure. I didn't know if I'd ever marry again; I had given up on the possibility of knowing true love.

question: When you think of retirement, what comes to mind?

answer: A coffin. This has been such an adventure. I've never had a grand scheme or plan for doing any of this; I simply went exploring and this is what happened. I never wanted to be bored.

HITTING HER STRIDE ▷ "If I'd known how good my fifties were going to be, I'd have gotten there long ago," laughs Phylicia Rashad. "I feel 17—only it's better now, because I know more. I like myself where I am. I wouldn't go back." Rashad has every reason to sit back and smile. Recently, she costarred with her sister, Debbie Allen, in *The Old Settler*, a play that aired on PBS. She also returned to her stage roots, starring in the off-Broadway play *Blue*. "Every day was like an acting lesson, and I love learning," she says. "I never want to stop."

Known to millions as Clair Huxtable, Bill Cosby's on-screen attorney wife on *The Cosby Show*, and as Cosby's "better half" on *Cosby*, Rashad is the recipient of two NAACP Image Awards for her work on those shows. She also earned two People's Choice Awards and was nominated twice for an Emmy. Despite accolades, she's still studying.

"I've taken Portuguese, hatha yoga, movement, and ballet, and I go to voice class," Rashad says, laughing. "I'll be learning until my last breath." Breathing is something she has studied very seriously—with the late guru Swami Muktananda, who, she says, "altered my life and showed me grace." Rashad meditates almost every day because it "puts things in a clearer perspective. I can appreciate each moment for what it is, no matter what."

Long before her guru guided her to inner peace, Rashad's mother had taken her on another kind of journey. "I was in eighth grade when Mother announced we were leaving 'this environment of ignorance'—Houston—for Mexico City," Rashad says. "I was truly angry, but that experience turned out to be one of the best and most wonderful things that ever happened to me." Rashad found in Mexico a "culture of many cultures that appreciated me for who I was and didn't care about the color of my skin."

{ "If I'd known how good my fifties were going to be, I'd have gotten there long ago." }

An honors graduate of Howard University, where she has also taught, Rashad began her acting career in the hit musicals *Jelly's Last Jam*, *Into the Woods*, and *The Wiz*. She won her role in *The Cosby Show* by "auditioning, just like everybody else. We had no idea what a hit it would be."

The actress, who is divorced, says that her greatest challenge and greatest joy remain her daughter, 14, and son, 28. "It's such a beautiful gift to be a mother," she explains. "My kids are part of the privileged life I've had." When Rashad reflects on where she is at midlife, she says, "I weep tears of gratitude because, at this age, I know each challenge has allowed me to grow. I've been given so much: a life full of texture and color, wonder and surprise. The fact that I'm still able to live in a meaningful, productive way—for that I am most grateful."

PHYLICIa

raSHaD

Occupation:
Actress
Born:
June 19, 1948

DIane

Occupation:
Newscaster
Born:
December 22, 1945

Sawyer

{Prime Time} Despite her intriguing resume, which begins in her teens, Diane Sawyer considers herself a late bloomer. One thing is certain: At 56, she is in her prime. One of America's most visible and respected network newswomen, Sawyer was inducted into the Academy of Television Arts and Sciences in 1997

"I really believed that eventually I would meet the right person and know it. And I did.

for her investigative reporting. She had captured fame early on. At 17, she was America's Junior Miss; at 22, a "weather-girl" for WLKY-TV in Kentucky; at 25, a White House press aide in the Nixon administration. Four years later, when Nixon resigned in 1974, she helped the beleaguered ex-president write his memoirs.

CBS News hired Sawyer in 1978, ultimately making her its State Department correspondent. Eleven years later, after coanchoring *The CBS Morning News* and being named the first woman reporter for *60 Minutes*, the brainy blond turned down a $10 million-a-year contract from Fox News to join ABC News for a reported $6 million per year. At around this time, she proposed to film director Mike Nichols, two years after meeting him in a Paris airport lounge. They married in 1988, when she was 42.

In addition to coanchoring ABC's *PrimeTime Thursday*, Sawyer often fills in for Peter Jennings on *World News Tonight* and for Ted Koppel on *Nightline*. Most recently, she has returned to her morning roots, rising at 4 a.m. each weekday to coanchor *Good Morning America* with Charles Gibson.

question: With your schedule, how do you keep in shape?

answer: It's hard, given the fact that I'm a slug by instinct! I lost more than 20 pounds with the help of Jim Karas, a fitness trainer who worked with me on a diet series for *Good Morning America*.

question: What, no self-destructive tendencies?

answer: If I could give you an example of something self-destructive, I would. I have some kind of New England stoicism with a Southern veneer.

question: You married in your early forties. Did you surprise yourself by getting married?

answer: It's about whether you believe there's one person out there. It probably looked insane on my part, but I really believed that eventually I would meet the right person and know it immediately. And I did. The first time I heard Mike talk, it was just so clear that he was surprising and hilarious. He wakes up in the middle of the night really funny. I knew I would never be bored.

question: Do you have any regrets that you haven't had children?

answer: What I decided was that I wanted Mike. He had children from two different marriages, and I loved them completely. To present him with another set of children didn't seem the right impulse. It wasn't that we didn't talk about it; we did, but it was late and we had this great thing and I also didn't want his children ever to feel that I had come in and changed their whole lives.

question: You're sometimes referred to as a late bloomer. Does this label bother you?

answer: I can't imagine what it would feel like if I had achieved everything at 25—if I had found the perfect man and the perfect job. Knowing me, I'd be throwing it all away for some guy in a mariachi band.

CELINDA

LAKE

Occupation:
Pollster, Strategist
Born:
April 13, 1953

making a difference ▷ "I have a lot of feelings about turning 50," says Celinda Lake, one of the Democratic Party's leading political strategists. "For one thing, I'm firmly established in what I do. I can look back at all I've been through and have a sense of security—that I have made it."

Lake is president of Lake Snell Perry & Associates, which she started in 1995 after working for a number of other polling firms. "Friends and coworkers kept telling me I should start my own business, but in my thirties, I really didn't have the confidence. That, too, came with age," she says. "Having my own company is the best thing I ever did." In seven years, her company has grown from five employees to 35.

One of the nation's top experts on electing women candidates and reaching women voters, Lake has been a pollster for candidates at all levels of government. She's assisted democratic political parties in Indonesia, South Africa, and Eastern Europe, and she is a pollster for *U. S. News and World Report.* Lake and her staff are known for their cutting-edge research on issues such as the economy, health care, the environment, and campaign finance reform. A 70-hour workweek is the norm for Lake, who is single.

{ "As I approach 50, I have had to adjust some of my expectations. But the payoff is that I love what I do." }

"As I approach 50, I have had to adjust some of my expectations," she says. "I don't know that I'll ever marry, and I probably won't have kids. I just don't have the time. But the payoff is that I love what I do—because we are working for causes that make a difference."

Lake, who says she was a "teenage Republican," graduated from Smith College in 1975 and planned to attend law school. But while taking a summer course at the University of Geneva, she met a group of Americans who were researching political behavior. Back at school, she wrote about their work and became "a changed person." In 1980, she returned to the United States and earned a master's degree from the University of Michigan. She had become a Democrat, too. "The women's movement and the Vietnam War had changed me," she explains.

One of Lake's goals as she turns 50 is to take more time off—she's an avid white-water rafter—and to spend more time with friends. "At this age, I've had friends who have died," she says. "I'm still here and grateful for that. I'm also cognizant that I have friends who have been in my life now for 25 or more years. I feel that's an important accomplishment—to say somebody has actually been a friend for more than 25 years."

renaissance woman ▷ Sandy Lerner, cofounder of Cisco Systems, walked

away with a cool $85 million when her company went public in 1990. She was 35. With more than half her life still ahead of her, the self-described nerd decided to embrace all of her interests. Since then, she has become a philanthropist, an entrepreneur, a farmer, an animal rights advocate, a medieval jouster, a restaurateur, and a preserver of rare books. What she hasn't become is preoccupied with heading toward 50.

"As long as I'm getting older, I'm still here," says Lerner. "The one thing I do know is that I'm a lot smarter than I used to be."

If so, Lerner's IQ must be off the chart. In 1984, while running a computer lab at Stanford, she and husband Len Bosack developed the first commercially viable router, the basis for a computer network. Soon afterward, Cisco Systems was born. Six years later she and Bosack left the company, splitting $170 million. Lerner was not entirely comfortable with her sudden wealth. "I have a healthy fear of money," she explains. "I decided not to let it run my life." To that end, Lerner and Bosack (now her ex-husband and best friend) started the Bosack-Kruger Charitable Foundation, which donates money to animal welfare organizations. The pair also developed PetNet, which provides humane societies with free software to link rescue efforts.

{ "The best thing about having all this money is I'm able to give back." }

"I grew up on a farm," says Lerner, who was raised by an aunt and uncle after her parents divorced when she was 4. "I spent most of my childhood alone, so I came to depend on animals. You can always count on them."

Lerner still surrounds herself with animals on Ayshire Farm, an 800-acre estate in northern Virginia where she lives in a two-room log cabin (the 40-room main house is used primarily for fund-raisers). A working organic farm, it's also home to several hundred farm animals, including Lerner's collection of shire horses. (She fell in love with these massive animals while participating in Renaissance-style jousting events.) Ayshire Farm employs 40 workers, including mentally and physically disabled people who might otherwise be unemployable.

The farm is not Lerner's first independent business venture. In 1995—because she dislikes pink—Lerner launched Urban Decay, a line of grunge-girl cosmetics (the dominant colors are green, blue, and purple) that found an eager audience. She sold the company two years ago and today devotes most of her energy to philanthropy. "The best thing about having all this money is I'm able to give back," she says. "To do that for the rest of my life is an enormous privilege."

Sandy

Lerner

Occupation:
Entrepreneur
Born:
August 14, 1955

IYANLA

Occupation:
Author, TV Host

Born:
September 13, 1953

vanzant

{An Inner Vision} In 49 years, Iyanla Vanzant has come a long way. Priestess, lawyer, best-selling author, television talk show host— she's a source of inspiration for millions. Born in the back of a taxi to an unwed mother, she suffered an abusive childhood, underwent a teenage pregnancy, and went on welfare after leaving a violent marriage. Determined to overcome the long odds, she worked her way through Medgar Evers College, graduating summa cum laude. (The same college awarded her an honorary doctorate in 1999.) Next, she attended law school at New York City's Queens

College and did doctoral studies at Temple University. Six of her 11 inspirational books, including *In the Meantime*, have been best-sellers, and she's sold more than 8 million books all told. In addition to writing, Vanzant is executive director of the Inner Visions Spiritual Life Maintenance Center in Silver Spring, Maryland. The center's goal is to infuse the world with love and healing through workshops and seminars. Familiar to many as a frequent guest on *Oprah*, Vanzant has her own daytime talk show, *Iyanla*, which was launched in August 2001. Ordained a Yoruba priestess at age 30, she has three children and four grandchildren. She is married to Adeyemi Bandele.

question: Are you afraid of turning 50?

answer: No. In fact I'm so excited I don't know what to do, because the closer I get to 50, the less I care about what others think. Before 40, I was always trying to impress somebody.

question: What's the most valuable lesson you've learned so far?

answer: That no matter how old I get, I have to enjoy my own company. At 20, I wanted somebody—anybody—to keep me company. In my thirties, I wanted to pick and choose my company. At 40, I began to question this need for company at all. Now, as I get close to 50, company can just go away. I need to enjoy not only my own physical company, but also be in touch with my thoughts and feelings, likes and dislikes. It's more important now to be in unity with myself, and to act on what I say.

question: How is married life?

answer: Adeyemi and I can't take each other for granted. We must make clear our efforts at keeping the energy of our marriage alive. We can't afford to go two weeks without doing something to boost our relationship. A marriage is a living thing. It needs attention, or it will die.

question: What is the most meaningful advice that you would offer to women as they approach the midlife years?

answer: Tell the truth. When you're getting older, you can't remember stuff, so if you always tell the truth, you don't have to worry about remembering what you said.

question: How about the most meaningful spiritual advice?

answer: Pay attention to what you're learning about yourself on the way. Spirituality doesn't mean an end to chaos or confusion or struggle. It doesn't mean I'm going to find a man or drive a "Beemer" or get to age 75 without having to wear an underwire bra. It means I'm OK with who I am all the time. I'm truly in the world, but it may not always be pretty.

50/50:

Iyanla
Vanzant

"SPIRITUALITY DOESN'T mean an end to chaos or confusion or STRUGGLE. IT means I'M OK WITH WHO I am all THE TIME."

Occupation:
Episcopal Priest
Born:
June 7, 1952

BETH

LONG

KEEPING THE FAITH ▷ Beth Long's journey to the Episcopal priesthood took some extraordinary twists and turns. Today, at 50, she says her spiritual journey is anything but over. Currently rector of Trinity Episcopal Church in Lime Rock, Connecticut, she has been married to Bill Burgower, a retired publisher, for 12 years.

"I haven't really thought about 50, other than in the sense that time is precious—even in terms of my spiritual experience.

"As far back as I can remember, I had an interest in spiritual life and the Bible. As a child I enjoyed church and would memorize hymns for my prayers. My parents were Lutheran and Roman Catholic, but they ultimately chose the Episcopal Church because of its religious tolerance and inclusiveness. At the University of Toronto, I majored in religious studies; in 1980, I got my master's in theology from St. Michaels University. I really didn't know what I wanted to do, but remember watching a Roman Catholic priest prepare to celebrate Mass and thinking, 'If I were a man, that's what I'd do.'

"I joined the Catholic Church in graduate school because I was drawn to its worship, its mystical teachings, and its traditions. Later, I joined a religious community, Sisters of Our Lady of Sion. The group is dedicated to helping Christians understand their Jewish roots.

"When I was 27, the Sisters asked me to go to Rome, where I had a spiritual awakening. I was on a silent retreat—sitting at lunch by myself. Suddenly, I had a very powerful experience: the realization that my life had always and only existed in the womb of God, the life of Christ. This was an experience of profound love, and I understood for the first time that life is stronger than death. From that moment, I knew that no matter what happened, I was not alone, and that God would always be with me.

"A few years later, I left the Order because I wanted to be married and have a family. My father's Episcopal priest kept nudging me to return to his church and to explore the ministry there. Eventually, I did. At 36, during the ordination process, I met my husband, who's Jewish, at a singles dance in a Unitarian church. We discovered we shared a mutual interest in spiritual life, and about a year later, we married.

"At 50, my challenge is to continue to face the unfathomable and not to use what I already know as a hedge against living in faith. It is joyful and deeply liberating to be faithful to what is true."

{ "It is joyful and deeply liberating to be faithful to what is true." }

PEGGY

Occupation:
Skater
Born:
July 27, 1948

FLEMING

survivor ▷ At age 19, figure skater Peggy Fleming, already the holder of three World Championships, became the only American to win a gold medal at the 1968 Winter Olympics. In 1970, she married Greg Jenkins, a dermatologist. Since then, she's had a professional skating career and has been a network sports commentator. Four years ago, she battled breast cancer. She lives in California with her husband; they have two sons and a grandson.

question: Do you miss skating and all the joys it brought?

answer: Today, simply being alive is a great joy. At 50, I was diagnosed with breast cancer and had a lumpectomy. On the thirtieth anniversary of winning the gold medal, I was undergoing an operation to see if the cancer had spread. Fortunately it hadn't. I underwent radiation and I'm fine. Then, two years ago, I lost my sister to a heart attack. She was only 50. I still can't believe she's gone. She was so young, just like my dad who died of a heart attack at 41.

{ "Know your body, take care of yourself, and treasure every moment." }

question: So death touched your life at a very early age?

answer: I was 17 when my father died. The only reason I was able to continue skating was through others' generosity. Mom had four girls to raise, and she sewed skating costumes to help supplement Dad's Social Security. She made the chartreuse dress I wore in the '68 Olympics for just $20. It's amazing that Mom and I managed my career so well. I didn't have a business manager or an agent.

question: You've been married 31 years. To what do you attribute this success?

answer: I honestly think the marriage works because we were apart so much. I traveled constantly, so we were always renewing the relationship. Our careers gave us the space we needed to be who we were. We have an enormous respect for one another.

question: At 54, you still have the skin of someone in her thirties. How did you manage that?

answer: Being married to a dermatologist certainly helped! I also wear sunscreen all the time and apply moisturizer right after every shower. I've had a bit of cosmetic surgery to smooth out the edges—the bags under my eyes removed, some Botox around the forehead and eyes. In this arena I think people should do what makes them happy.

question: Do you have any special thoughts about having passed the half-century mark?

answer: Fifty seems so much more serious than 40; it's more challenging to stay healthy and in shape. Maybe I've been singled out to survive so I can be the one to say, "Know your body, take care of yourself, and treasure every moment."

amy

Occupation:
Author
Born:
February 19, 1952

{Joy and Luck} Parents play a crucial role in all our lives—but it's safe to say that Daisy Tan has had a greater influence than most. She inspired her daughter, best-selling author Amy Tan, to invent a new genre of women's fiction that began with the 1989 publication of *The Joy Luck Club.* The book, which drew heavily on both Daisy's life in China and the tumultuous relationship Amy Tan had with her mother, zoomed to the top of the best-seller lists, transforming

"IT WOULD'VE BEEN karma HAD I ENDED UP WITH a DAUGHTER as

Amy Tan into a household name. But it wasn't until her mid-thirties that Tan sought to resolve her conflicted and sometimes torturous relationship with her mother, who died of Alzheimer's in 1999. One way was *The Bonesetter's Daughter*, the novel she published last year, which helped her to finally exorcise the lingering demons from her past. Today, Tan and her husband, retired tax lawyer Lou DeMattei, live in San Francisco with Lilli and Bubba, their beloved Yorkshire terriers.

question: Your mother's story—an abusive first marriage that produced three sisters you never met, hardships in World War II China, your grandmother's suicide—ended up as the foundation for both *The Joy Luck Club* and *The Kitchen God's Wife*. How did you react when you first found out about her past?

answer: I ultimately reacted by finding friends who were existentially fed up with life and their parents, who'd tuned in to drugs, who rejected society. My friends were jailed, then deported because my mother had provided evidence for their convictions. My goal was to escape living with her.

question: Why did you reconcile?

answer: It was 1986. My mother was hospitalized with heart attack symptoms. When I found out, I was sure I'd lost her; and then I wondered, what had I lost? It seemed even sadder that I didn't know the answer. So I vowed that if she lived, I'd get to know her better and even take her to China. When I reached my mother at the hospital, she laughed with delight to hear how worried I was! She told me she had not had a heart attack after all—that she'd had chest pains caused by her anger at a man at the fish market who was mean to her. But I could hear the voice of my conscience reminding me of my vow. So I took her to China and I started to write fiction in an effort to see her from her own point of view.

question: Your mother died of Alzheimer's. Do you worry you might inherit it?

answer: Sure. Whenever I get stuck in writing or can't get through a book others have claimed as a

DIFFICULT TO me AS I WAS TO MY MOTHER.

masterpiece, I'm sure this is diagnostic.

question: Your mother was very superstitious. Did she pass that along to you?

answer: My mother believed I was a conduit, a channel. She used to have me use a Ouija board to try to contact our departed relatives. I grew up resenting, even hating the notion of ghosts and such things; now they're a part of my life. I do believe life continues in some way. I call it a spirit.

question: Ever regret not having children?

answer: It would've been karma had I ended up with a daughter as difficult to me as I was to my mother. I don't know if I could've gone through that kind of heartbreak.

carole owens

Occupation:
Talent Coordinator
Born:
June 13, 1948

a HEALING LEGACY ▷ Carole Owens, a talent coordinator for a New York City television station, is the mother of Joseph, 16, and Damoria, 32; she is also a grandmother. When she was 44, her 22-year-old son, Ryan, was killed, an innocent bystander caught in the cross fire of a street fight. Since then, she's found that helping others has helped her heal.

"At 50, you definitely have a better idea of who you are and who you want to be—though in many ways, I still feel like I'm growing up. My son's death, no doubt, plays a part in that feeling.

"It was March 31, 1993, when it happened. After watching his favorite TV shows, Ryan had walked to our neighborhood deli in Queens for his usual late-night snack—a tuna on raisin toast. There was an argument outside the store. Shots were fired, people inside hit the floor, and when it was over everybody got up but Ryan. He died the next day.

"Six hundred people came to his funeral. During that period, some of my friends actually moved into my house to help me through my grief. My door was always open, because people kept coming to talk about him. He was a loving and caring boy about to embark on a new phase in life. He had a girlfriend and was set to enter college that fall.

{ "Grief can make you so weary. But when you can forgive and let go of the hurt, you can start to heal." }

"Everybody said I was so strong. But that wasn't it at all. If I hadn't had my faith, I would have lost my mind. A couple of years after Ryan's death, I formed a prayer group with three other people at my church. We pray separately and together for those who are sick, lonely, or in any way in need of comfort.

"It's interesting that, more often than not, I find myself in the company of people who are in need of emotional healing due to the death of a loved one. If they want to talk, I listen, and it seems to help. Grief can make you so weary. But when you can forgive and let go of the hurt, you can start to heal.

"I don't think you ever really get over losing a child—and, to be honest, I sometimes still ask myself why it happened. But I have to trust that God knows more than I do. Ryan was, after all, His child. I think about him most on his birthday; I always wonder what kind of man he would have been. It was a privilege to have known him.

"Because of his death, I've met people I never might have known and have sometimes been able to help them in wondrous and miraculous ways. As painful as this experience was, I'm much stronger and much wiser now."

WHAT AN ANGEL! ▷

Just shy of 50, Arlene Untenberg expanded her business, "Angels…A Celestial Gathering Place," in Milford, Connecticut. This unusual shop now offers its customers gourmet coffee and holistic health treatments. A true angel acolyte, Untenberg surrounds herself with the heavenly creatures both at home (where she has a private collection) and at work (her shop sells thousands), and she is delighted when customers share their angel experiences. Married twice, Untenberg is the mother of two: a son, 29, and a daughter, 27.

"As I was about to hit 50 and in the midst of trying to open my expanded store, my husband lost his job and then my mother died. It was a difficult time, but I knew I'd be OK because of an experience I had 8 years earlier, when my mother-in-law died of pancreatic cancer. Witnessing her death changed my life; it put me in touch with my angels.

"Before I opened my shop, I had been an X-ray technician. I'd seen other people die, but my mother-in-law's passing was different. She was in a coma-like state on her last day in the hospital, but I could feel her presence, out of her body, in the room. When she took her last breath, her eyes rolled back. As a group of us stood at her bedside, saying our goodbyes, something strange happened. Her eyes rolled back down and focused on each of us, one at a time. Having her look at me was one of the most emotional experiences I've ever had.

{ "Angels are all around us; they just want to be asked in. And when that happens, they start guiding us." }

"The experience brought back all of the Catholic beliefs I had been raised with, but always questioned. Soon, I began keeping a journal, and ultimately my spiritual path opened up. Until then, I felt I'd been sleepwalking through life. I'd been happy, but not necessarily fulfilled. When I got in touch with my angels, I knew where I needed to go. It's difficult to say how it happens—it's like an inner voice, or getting the chills when you know something is right. Angels are all around us; they just want to be asked in. And when that happens, they start guiding us.

"At the end of 1994, I opened a shop that sold angels and angel items. I also went through hospice training. I had found my higher purpose: helping people and their loved ones in the 'crossing over' process.

"The angels also led me to expand my store into another realm. Today, the store offers therapeutic services of all kinds, from hypnosis to massage.

"At this point in my life, things seem to have come together. It's almost like I spent the first 50 years climbing up the mountain. On the other side, I've found joy."

arLene

Occupation:
Angel Expert
Born:
April 24, 1950

unrenBerg

DON'T CALL ME MADAM

▷ At 32, Sydney Biddle Barrows was arrested for operating a Manhattan escort service that reportedly took in more than $1 million a year. Dubbed the Mayflower Madam because of her blue-blood lineage, she became instantly infamous. Today this woman with a past wants it to be history. She's building a new image for herself as an expert in the art of cosmetic surgery and has a book in progress on the subject.

"Fifty is so different for me," says Barrows, who's undergone liposuction and a facelift and has had her eyes done. "Thirty was traumatic; at 40, I thought I had no future. Now, I'm really taking care of myself." Barrows sighs as she recalls "that time in my life when I couldn't go places or do things without people whispering. I had made an unfortunate choice in life, and people wouldn't let me forget."

The story of that choice began at the unemployment office. "I'd lost my retailing job," she explains. "While in line, I met a girl who was making $50 a night answering phones for an escort service." It was 1978, and to the 26-year-old Barrows, struggling to pay her rent, it sounded great. "One thing led to another, and soon I was answering phones," says the preppy descendant of Pilgrims. "I knew I could do a better job, so I set up my own service."

Barrows's first book, *Mayflower Madam*, which helped pay her legal bills, was made into a movie starring Candice Bergen. A stint on the speakers' circuit followed, along with two other books. Then she hit the Big Four-O.

"On my fortieth birthday, I started crying and cried for two weeks," she says. "At this point, I always thought I'd be married and have a nice home, a good career. I had none of these things." That's when she decided to make some changes.

"I was grossly overweight. At 5'6" I weighed 173 pounds. The day I tried on a size 14 and it was too tight, I said, 'That's it,' and rejoined a gym." As her body changed, she grew more confident. And "reporters stopped calling me every time a madam was busted. That was the biggest relief." At 41, she met "a nice man who wasn't bothered by my baggage." At 42, they married. At 46, she had a facelift.

Today, Barrows is at work on her fourth book, *Getting a Little Work Done*, a consumer guide to cosmetic surgery. "When people think about changing their image, I want them to think of my book. I hope this is what people will remember me for."

{ "Thirty was traumatic; at 40, I thought I had no future. Now, I'm really taking care of myself." }

SYDNEY

Occupation:
Author
Born:
January 14, 1952

BIDDLE Barrows

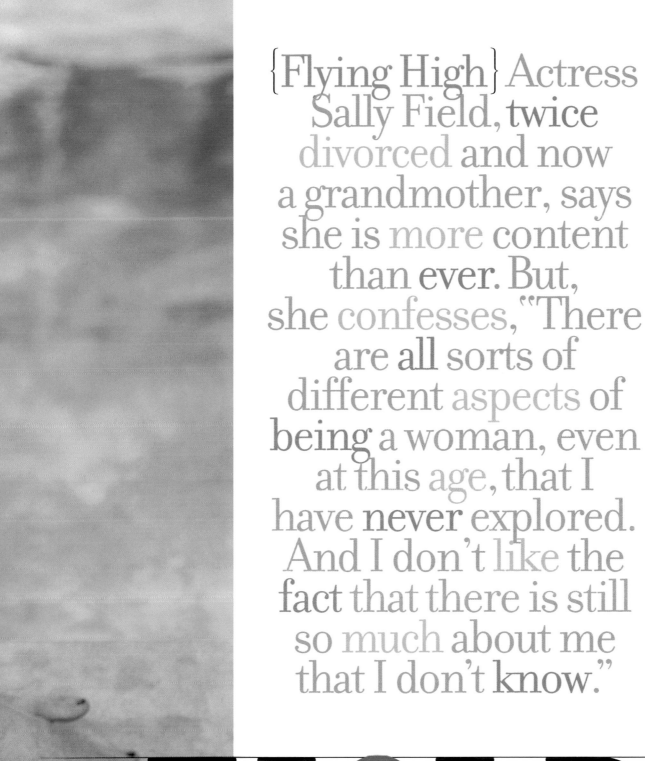

{Flying High} Actress Sally Field, twice divorced and now a grandmother, says she is more content than ever. But, she confesses, "There are all sorts of different aspects of being a woman, even at this age, that I have never explored. And I don't like the fact that there is still so much about me that I don't know."

SALLY

FIELD

Occupation:
Actress, Director
Born:
November 6, 1946

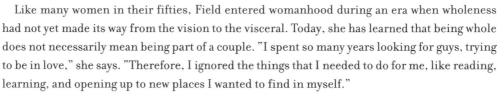

Like many women in their fifties, Field entered womanhood during an era when wholeness had not yet made its way from the vision to the visceral. Today, she has learned that being whole does not necessarily mean being part of a couple. "I spent so many years looking for guys, trying to be in love," she says. "Therefore, I ignored the things that I needed to do for me, like reading, learning, and opening up to new places I wanted to find in myself."

One of the new places she's discovered is the other side of the camera. In 2000, Field, who made her name early on with such television classics as *Gidget* and *The Flying Nun*, directed *Beautiful*, her first feature-length motion picture. She looks forward, she says, to sitting in the director's chair again. That's no surprise, perhaps, coming from a woman who describes herself as "hugely competitive"—an attribute that has served the once-shy actress well.

Stymied by the giddy roles she played early in her career, Field was turned down for a chance to audition for the title role in *Sybil*, a film about a woman with multiple personalities. She showed up anyway, refusing to leave until she was given the opportunity to read. Her persistence paid off; she not only won the role, but also a 1976 Emmy for her performance. Over the next

THere are all sorts of different aspects

decade, she would win Best Actress Oscars for 1979's *Norma Rae* and 1984's *Places in the Heart*.

A confirmed single woman who proclaims she no longer even likes the institution of marriage, Field is the mother of two grown sons, Peter, 33, and Elijah, 30, from her marriage to high school sweetheart Steve Craig. (She was actually pregnant during the final season of *The Flying Nun*.) She's also mom to Sam, 14, whose dad is producer Alan Greisman; that marriage ended in 1994.

Field's professional and personal experiences have helped her come to terms with insecurities that have plagued her, she says, for much of her life. "My generation of women has always grappled with how likable we have to be," she explains. "Deep down, we feel that certain things aren't acceptable—being driven, being obsessed." The actress's newfound stability is woven into the fabric of her life today. When not filming, she cooks dinner for Sam, helps with homework, and frequently visits Peter and his wife, Amy, who recently presented Field with her second granddaughter. Professionally, she made a triumphant return to television on *ER*, winning critical acclaim for her portrayal of a woman suffering from manic depression.

Being in her fifties has given Field the ability to "see in the distance." With age, she says, she has learned that no matter what happens, she can call on past experiences not only to survive, but to thrive. "Maturity comes when you can embrace your past on some terms," she explains. "Then you can move on to find other parts of yourself."

OF BEING A woman, even at THIS AGE, THAT I HAVE never EXPLORED.”

LIZ

culumber

reMODELING a LIFE ▷ At 40, Liz Cullumber found what she'd been looking for: her biological mother. Adopted at birth, Cullumber says the event opened her life to new possibilities. She entered the workforce for the first time at 41, later earning a master's degree and becoming a speech pathologist. That was just the beginning. Recently, at 52, Cullumber competed against 6,000 entrants and won a $15,000 modeling contract, first prize in the *MORE* Magazine/Wilhelmina search for models over 40. She left her teaching position to model full-time. Cullumber and her husband, Denis, a housing developer, live in the Los Angeles area and have two daughters, Amy, 31, and Katherine, 28.

"My distinctive look is my short white hair. I began coloring it at 26 when it first turned gray. Back then, the color wasn't fashionable. After I met my birth mother, my hair was the first of many things that I changed. I searched for her for years; then I hired a search consultant who found her in three days. At our first meeting, we stared at each other for what seemed an eternity. She had this beautiful white hair. We looked so alike it was uncanny—our mannerisms, our personalities, our voices. Finally, I had something physical I could relate to. I immediately let my hair go natural.

"We saw each other a lot and became friends. It wasn't the same bond I had shared with my adoptive mother. She died 11 years ago, and I'm thankful for all she did. But knowing my birth mother gave me closure. I was able to make peace and get on with my life. I'm not sure my birth mother was ever able to do that. She had me at 23. I was her big secret; she told no one, though after our initial meeting she did share me with my half brother and half sister.

{ "I actually dreaded being 50. But then it happened, and my life has never been better." }

"After meeting her, I started teaching. I had never worked outside the home. I grew up when feminism was in its infancy. Working appealed to me, but I was programmed to get married and have children.

"When she died in April 2001, they invited me to be at her bedside. It was extraordinary—she had been at my birth, and I at her death. But at her memorial service, no mention was made of me, that was heartbreaking. Still, I am grateful to have found her. At 40, I finally know who I was.

"A friend suggested I enter the *MORE* model contest, and I was stunned when I won. I had tired of teaching but didn't know what else to do. It's all been so exciting; I really love modeling.

"I actually dreaded being 50. But then it happened, and my life has never been better. It's gratifying to live in a time when women have so many choices—choices my birth mother didn't have."

a new american FAMILY ▷

As she turns 50 in 2002, Boston attorney Laura Carroll is grateful she was able to have children, despite never having found "the right guy." Adoptive mother to Louisa, 10, and Annalin, 6, she conceived her third child, James, 3, through in vitro fertilization when she was 45.

"I cannot imagine life without my children," she says. "I have single friends who are going through menopause suddenly realizing, 'Oh dear, I forgot to have kids.' I tell anyone who's waiting for Mr. Right to come along to keep in mind that it just might never happen."

The oldest of four children, Carroll graduated from the University of California at Santa Barbara in 1973, then went on to get a master's in Soviet studies and a law degree from Harvard. She always thought she'd marry and have children, but the timing never seemed right. "I turned down my college boyfriend's proposal; he simply didn't share my life's vision," she explains. By 1976, as she entered law school, her next serious boyfriend envisioned her staying at home. "Obviously, he was the wrong guy," she says. "Why would I be going to Harvard Law if I weren't serious about my career?"

In 1991, while visiting Costa Rica, Carroll met a pregnant teen looking for someone to adopt her baby. "I came home and looked for parents. None materialized," Carroll says. "The girl then confided she wanted me to adopt her baby; she felt sad I didn't have children. I remember hanging up the phone and thinking God was putting a baby right in my lap. How could I say no?"

Eventually, Carroll "decided to adopt again. I really wanted Louisa to know the joy of a sibling." But by then there was a moratorium on adoptions in Costa Rica. So on New Year's Eve 1995, Carroll went to China to pick up Annalin, a tiny and malnourished 5-month-old baby. "We bonded immediately," she says, "because I was the lady with the food."

Over the years, Carroll always had hoped to have a biological child. Finally, she decided to undergo in vitro fertilization using donor sperm. On October 5, 1998, her son James was born. "He's been a great addition to the family," she says happily. "The girls love him."

Perhaps surprisingly, the issue of finding a father rarely arises. "The children have so many friends whose parents are divorced," says Carroll. "They see how that impacts the kids. They'd rather see me as a single mom than a divorced one."

"I enjoy being with my children so much," Carroll says. "They keep me young. In fact, nobody believes I'm 50. I look 40. Children do that to you."

{ "I tell anyone who's waiting for Mr. Right to come along to keep in mind that it just might never happen." }

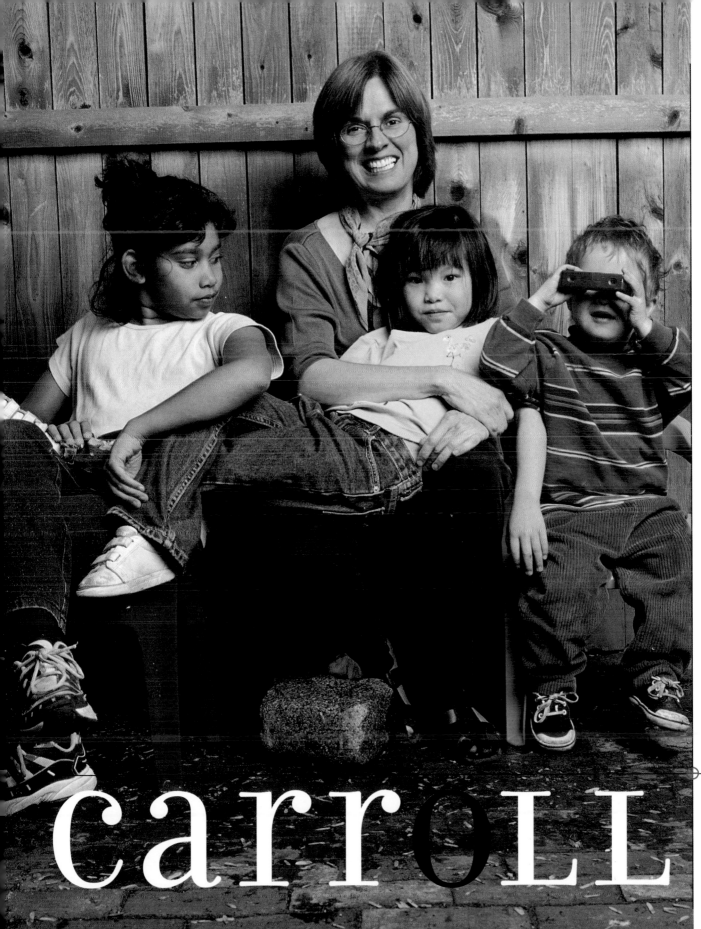

LAURA

CARROLL

Occupation:
Attorney
Born:
August 25, 1952

Occupation:
Chaplain, Mentor
Born:
January 11, 1948

maDELINE

manning mims

{Running Ahead} Fourteen national titles in track and field, an Olympic gold medal in 1968 and a silver in 1972: Madeline Manning Mims won them all. But throughout her life, there were other times she ran—not for glory, but for safety. In her early twenties, she fled an abusive husband; in 1972, she ran from terrorists in Munich. And although her life is much calmer today, Mims says she's still running to keep abreast of her many activities. With an honorary doctorate

"MY greatest accomplishment, however, remains my

of divinity from Oral Roberts Univesity, she heads the Ambassadorship, Inc., which mentors young athletes, and also serves as an Olympic chaplain. Mims lives in Tulsa with her husband, Roderick, and her mother, Queen L. Saulsberry, who suffers from Alzheimer's. Mims has two children: John, 31, and Lana, 14.

"People tell me I don't look like I'm in my fifties, probably because I exercise. I don't work out just to look good; I do it to feel good too. But I wasn't always so healthy.

"At age 3, I was diagnosed with spinal meningitis. When doctors told my mother I probably wouldn't survive, she prayed all night and essentially gave me back to the Lord. The next morning, I improved, but doctors warned I'd probably be mentally or physically disabled. My mother just looked at them and said, 'I don't think so.'

"As a little girl, I was sickly and anemic—but when I wasn't ill, I was running. In the projects where I grew up in Cleveland, everybody ran. You had to get away from the gangs. In high school, I had a real gift for sports and was offered an athletic scholarship to Tennessee State College.

"I always demanded a lot from myself. Sometimes, before a meet, I'd cry to release tension. But then I would remember that I wasn't running for me, but for Jesus. I have always felt He was by my side.

"Knowing that was especially important to me when my first husband and I divorced—and also the following year, when I witnessed the greatest tragedy in Olympic history. During the 1972 games in Munich, I was housed next to the Israeli dorm when it was attacked by terrorists.

"We didn't know for sure what was happening until a group of us went onto our balcony and saw hooded sharpshooters on the roof of the adjacent building. When we tried to run back inside, the door jammed. We were petrified. Later, we learned 11 hostages had been taken from the Olympic Village and killed at the airport. I kept that memory buried inside me for years.

FAMILY. FOR THEM, I AM MOST GRATEFUL.

Writing about it in my autobiography finally helped me to heal.

"I've also tried to help others heal in their lives by creating a mentoring program for women in prison. In the last few years, I've served as a chaplain working with athletes at the Olympic Games, giving them encouragement and strengthening their spirit to always perform their best. My ministry reaches out to young people in the performing arts in this same way.

"My greatest accomplishment, however, remains my family. For them, I am most grateful. And if I don't look 50, I don't act like it either. That's what happens when you have a 14-year-old around. She really keeps me running!"

TAPESTRY OF LIFE ▷ While her friends pursued high-powered careers, Susan Khalje followed her own path, part of a new generation of women eager to explore the world and live and work far from home. Raised on a Maryland tree farm, Khalje studied piano through childhood and college. But it was a high school sewing class that would determine the tapestry of her life, ultimately leading her to Afghanistan. Author of two books on design and sewing, she's finishing up a third; she also hosts HGTV's *Sew Much More*. She and her husband, Qadir, live outside Baltimore with their children, Soraya, 22, and Sharif, 18.

"I always believed 50 would bring some kind of shift, but I always related it to possibly returning to Afghanistan. Never, ever did I think I'd be making my debut as a television host, talking about sewing of all things. Though music was my first love—I taught piano for a while in London—I'd always sewed. Since earning a living as a musician wasn't easy, I took a job at a small couture house in New York. Little did I realize that what I learned there would help shape my life.

"A couple of years later, a friend offered me the opportunity to design a clothing line and supervise its manufacture in Afghanistan. A month after moving, I fell madly, deeply in love, not only with the country but with one of its citizens. I met Qadir on a Monday, and by Thursday we knew. We married less than six months later, in March 1978.

"We never dreamed what would await us. While Russian troops massed on the Afghan border, I learned I was pregnant. Qadir became ill, was hospitalized, and got typhoid. The political situation worsened. I got an exit visa and drove through the Khyber Pass to Pakistan. When Qadir got stronger, he joined me. Returning to the United States was another nightmare: U.S. officials confused Qadir with another man who had been charged with a crime, and he was denied entry. Ultimately his name was cleared.

"We made our home on the farm where I grew up, and I began designing and sewing wedding gowns. I also taught, and eventually was asked to write a book about couture gowns. Another book followed. A producer saw the books and called about hosting a show. The show premiered October 8, 2001—one month after my fiftieth birthday. I still can't believe it.

"I dream of returning one day to Afghanistan and sharing Qadir's heritage with our children. Though that possibility seems dim, who knows? At this stage, life is a series of surprises."

{ "I dream of returning one day to Afghanistan. Who knows? At this stage, life is a series of surprises." }

Susan

KHALJE

Occupation:
Author, TV Host
Born:
September 2, 1951

OH BABY! ▷ She was the ultimate Seventies supermodel, an all-American beauty who appeared to have it all. However, behind the smiling image of cover girl Cheryl Tiegs was a woman searching for inner peace and a sense of family. She found both after turning 50. "Fifty was a piece of cake," laughs Tiegs, who at the time was a thrice-divorced mom of a 6-year-old son. "It was 51 that hit me."

Born in Minnesota and raised in California, Tiegs appeared on *Glamour*, her first national magazine cover, in 1964. She dropped out of college at 20 and moved to Manhattan to model full-time. Over the next decade, she became the icon of wholesome, sun-drenched American style. Graduation to sexy siren came in 1970, when *Sports Illustrated* showcased her in its annual swimsuit edition (she continued to model for the annual issues up to the age of 47). She was a pioneer in lucrative long-term product-endorsement deals and was one of the first celebrities to lend her name to a clothing line, in her case for Sears.

Tiegs's private life was not as successful. In 1970, she married director Stan Dragoti, dropped out of modeling, and put on 35 pounds. Within two years, she'd lost the weight and revived her career. Dragoti struggled with drug addiction, and the couple divorced in 1979. Two years later, she married wildlife photographer Peter Beard; that union came to an end in 1983. By then she'd met Anthony Peck, a screenwriter who'd followed his famous father into the film industry. They married and, in 1991, after several miscarriages, Tiegs gave birth to a son, Zack, now 10. But in 1995 this marriage, too, dissolved, under the stress of Peck's addiction to pills and alcohol.

{ "If you calm your breath, you calm your mind. To calm the mind is to calm the system." }

For the first time in her life, the supermodel was alone. She retreated to the solitude of a Santa Barbara beach house with her son. "The idea of me on my own was so scary," she confesses. "But I was wrong. I feel more confident and secure because of that experience." Much of her inner happiness today is due to meditation, yoga, and learning how to breathe. "Breathing is a reflection of the mind," she says. "If you calm your breath, you calm your mind. That helps alleviate stress and works on the nervous system. To calm the mind is to calm the system."

Tiegs's study of yoga led to another life-changing event: her 1998 marriage to yoga instructor Rod Stryker. With the help of a surrogate, they became parents of twin sons Theo and Jaden, now 2. "It's important to have your own identity—and to let your kids see that," she says.

CHERYL

TIEGS

Occupation:
Model
Born:
September 25, 1947

JUDY

Occupation:
Newscaster
Born:
November 20, 1946

{Inside Politics} From the Carter administration to the second Bush presidency, CNN anchor and senior correspondent Judy Woodruff has reported on every national political convention and presidential campaign since 1976. She's also covered Washington politics for the *MacNeil/Lehrer News Hour* and for NBC News. Winner of numerous journalism awards, she cofounded the International Women's Media Foundation, which

WOODRUFF

I now tell people what I think, and have stopped trying to make everybody happy.

promotes women in communications worldwide. She lives in Washington, D.C., with her husband, *Wall Street Journal* executive Washington editor Al Hunt, and their three children, ages 13 to 20.

question: There are so few women in their fifties on network newscasts. Do you think it will ever get better for older women?

answer: The women you see now are among that first wave who hit television news in the Seventies. Since more women have entered the business, you will eventually begin to see more older women, especially on the networks, where credibility is so important. This isn't entertainment, which is fixated on youth. Of course, this trend may not always be reflected in local newscasts, where, in most parts of the country, it's been said anchor teams look like "a husband and his second wife." But you have to look at the overall improvement. Today, more than half of the anchors are women.

question: Had you achieved most of your goals by the time you turned 50?

answer: Actually, I'm much further along than I ever dreamed. As I approached 50, I thought the banana peel was in front of me and that I would go splat, down some hole. But there was also a part of me that thought life would get more interesting. I had friends in their fifties who had such interesting lives. They even tended to get smarter. I certainly feel braver and far more willing to take risks. I now tell people what I think, and have stopped trying to make everybody happy.

question: What's been your greatest challenge?

answer: Dealing with my older son's brain injury. He was born with a mild form of spina bifida, a neural tube defect. Though he had some minor issues, he was doing well—working at grade level in school. He ran, swam, even skied. Then, four years ago when he was 16, he underwent an operation to change a brain shunt, and there was an accident. As a result, he's unable to speak clearly, eat, or walk by himself. It changed every aspect of my life. He has a full-time companion who helps him and takes him to school.

question: How do you deal with this setback?

answer: I cried a lot of tears for a long time. I don't think you ever get over something like this, but it's certainly set my priorities in motion. I feel more keenly and intensely the importance of family, friends, and the human community. This is when you learn what friendship truly is.

question: Your job is so demanding. Do you ever feel guilty you can't be with your family more?

answer: Fortunately, my travel is limited—and though the job is grueling, my husband is totally supportive of my career. My family knows I love them. But I do feel guilty all the time. I live with the notion I'm never going to be 100 percent at anything. And if that's not good enough, then CNN and my family are just going to have to fire me.

50/50:

Judy
Woodruff

Leap-year Baby ▷

Technically speaking, not everyone born in 1952 is celebrating a fiftieth birthday in 2002. Why? 1952 was a leap year. Baby boomers born February 29 of that year can claim to have recently celebrated their twelfth birthday. For Kathy Werther-Kapsy, one of these leap-year babies, life has been a series of opportunities, rebirths, and second chances.

"I turn 50 this year and will finally get my master's degree. While I'm happy with my academic accomplishments, I'm not so happy with the way I ran the first half of my life. Some of that had to do with drinking. The alcohol was alluring, and the desire to party was addicitve. I believe my greatest achievement was giving up alcohol in my late twenties, and I thank God every day that I can make up for the things I botched.

"I got pregnant at 17. Back then, you didn't talk about birth control or sex. You just did it. Even so, I was determined to get an education. My desire to learn is overwhelming.

"By 21, I had a second son, and four years later I began taking college courses. I also worked selling Avon products and clerking in a grocery store. I never stopped; I did too much. After 17 years, my husband and I called it quits—though we have a nice relationship now as grandparents. The divorce was mostly my fault; I was too busy finding out who I was. I wish I'd focused more on my family. Fortunately, I've been given a second chance.

"Eight years ago, I married a wonderful man I met at a singles dance. I also went back to college full-time and finally got my bachelor's degree, in professional communications. My second husband and I had a baby—this time a girl, Tess. I feel blessed; I've been given the opportunity to try and do it right. Now, I have the special task of raising a daughter to be a responsible, compassionate, and assertive woman.

{ "Maybe I've achieved a lot—at least for someone who's technically only 12." }

"I am currently working on my master's degree. I also drive a school bus. Tess has been riding with me since she was 18 months old. When I hang up my bus keys, I hope to work from home so I can be there if she needs me. I also dabble in photography and do volunteer work. I was the first woman president of the local Lions club. I think, too, about writing children's books and getting my Ph.D.

"Sometimes I am disheartened to realize I haven't accomplished very much, particularly in comparison to people who have made tremendous contributions to humanity. Then again, I say to myself, maybe I've achieved a lot—at least for someone who's technically only 12."

KaTHY

WeRTHeR-KaPSY

Occupation:
Bus Driver, Student

Born:
February 29, 1952

JODY

Occupation:
Peace Activist
Born:
October 9, 1950

WILLIAMS

MAKING PEACE ▷ "You might say that I couldn't save my brother, so I've tried to save the world," says Jody Williams, winner of the 1997 Nobel Prize for Peace. As a founding coordinator of the International Campaign to Ban Landmines (ICBL), Williams, 51, coordinated efforts that culminated in the 1997 Mine Ban Treaty.

Trying to understand others' cruelty toward her brother—who was born deaf and later was diagnosed as schizophrenic—left Williams bewildered. "Our entire life—mine and my family's—was affected by his disability," notes Williams, who grew up in rural Vermont. "We were always looking for the right place to help him. I never understood how people could be so mean just because he was different."

In an attempt to combat the injustice she found on home turf, Williams began her fight for a kinder world. She's spent the last decade focusing her attention on a hidden enemy: the estimated 60 million landmines that lurk beneath the soil, mostly in rural areas where farmers plant and children play. Just as threatening, she says, are the world's more than 250 million stockpiled landmines.

> { "You might say I couldn't save my brother, so I've tried to save the world." }

Williams is delighted with her Nobel—and with the $1 million in prize money, which she split equally with the ICBL. But she says, "The prize certainly doesn't define me. My work says who I am. But since I don't take a salary, the money helps me live." (Because of taxes, nearly half of Williams's prize money went to the U.S. government—a sad irony in light of the fact that the United States didn't sign the 1997 treaty.)

Williams's earliest activist stirrings came during her days as a student at the University of Vermont, where she marched to protest the war in Vietnam. After earning a master's degree in international relations from Johns Hopkins, she went to Central America, primarily El Salvador and Nicaragua. It was there that she learned about the dangers of landmines. Today, as Williams continues her work with the ICBL, she dreams of taking a long vacation someday to nowhere in particular. "My husband keeps threatening to take me to Hawaii, but I travel so much that, one day, I'd just like to go as far as my dog can walk me," she laughs. She has begun to write poetry and plans to write "more personal stuff" in the future.

Williams is also hoping to find "an appropriate place" to display the Nobel medal and leather-bound original artwork she was awarded in Norway. For the time being, they grace the interior of a hall closet.

CATHY

Occupation:
Cartoonist
Born:
September 5, 1950

GUISEWITE

{Drawing on Experience} After graduating from the University of Michigan in 1972 with a degree in English, Cathy Guisewite began a career in advertising. To the delight of her mother, she was an immediate success—but dating was another story. Much to the amusement of her friends and family, Guisewite began creating cartoons that starred an angst-ridden single woman whose experiences were a reflection of her own. Four years later,

"One THING I LIKe aBOUT BEING 50 IS THaT THe pressure IS OFF. I Have earneD THe rIGHT TO reLax.

at her mother's insistence, the budding cartoonist submitted her work to Universal Press Syndicate. The strip struck a chord, and, within a week, the petite brunette had a contract. Today, *Cathy* is syndicated in more than 1,400 newspapers. The character's likeness has appeared in books, on products ranging from underwear to coffee mugs, and in television specials. (In 1987, the first animated *Cathy* won an Emmy.) And although the heroine of single women everywhere has yet to get hitched, *Cathy*'s creator married screenwriter/director Chris Wilkinson in November 1997, at the age of 47. The couple live in Los Angeles with Ivy, 9, the daughter Guisewite adopted when she was 41, and Wilkinson's son Cooper, 6.

"For my fiftieth birthday, my dream was to have my parents and two sisters visit. We're incredibly close but live in different parts of the country. Not only did my husband coordinate and arrange every detail for their trips, but he cooked this wonderful meal.

"Until I met Chris, I considered myself a complete package. I had a full and fulfilling life, a wonderful job, and a beautiful daughter. Despite what I depict in my comic strip, I was truly a committed single person. But by our second date, I was crazy about him; Chris felt the same way [about me]. We married a little more than a year after meeting at a dinner party. Just like my art, my life is built on contradictions. I was this happy single person, but I also had a complete fantasy wedding in my head—one I'd envisioned since age 5. It was so beautiful. I had a gorgeous dress and a puffy white veil.

"At 35, I actually had announced that I never wanted to marry or have kids. My mom, who had an entire box of wedding silver she'd been collecting since my birth, gave it to me anyway as if to say, 'We support your choice, but you may as well eat your single-serving microwave dinner with a silver fork.'

"Being married has helped the cartoon, giving me much more insight into how men think. Their relationship with football is so far beyond what I've made fun of in the comic strip, and I had no idea how little interest they had in shopping. We do inhabit different universes.

"It's safe to say Cathy will never marry. I was single for five hundred years and remember dating all too well. I also know the feeling of eating a low-fat bran muffin and wondering how much exercise you'll have to do to make up for it. I hope Cathy lasts a long time, that she will keep having a place. As long as manufacturers continue to make swimsuits the way they do, I think there'll be a need for her public outcry.

"One thing I like about being 50 is that the pressure is off to look and dress a certain way. It's not a giving up, but rather a giving in; it's a relief to no longer have to measure up to a ridiculous standard of beauty. I have earned the right to relax and know that everything will be OK. There's a certain peace about it. It really feels like a new phase of life, and I'm happy with it."

50/50:
Cathy
Guisewite

BEVERLY

JOHNSON

IN VOGUE ▷ The first African-American to appear on the cover of *Vogue*, in 1974, Beverly Johnson has been described as "the Jackie Robinson of the modeling world." But even though many consider Johnson an icon, her world doesn't begin or end in fashion. She has appeared in movies and on television, written three books on beauty, and developed lines of skin care products, eyewear, and a wig collection, all of which bear her name. Twice divorced, Johnson lives in California and is a golf enthusiast. Her daughter, Anansa, is 22.

"I cannot tell you how happy I am at this point in my life. I get up with a smile on my face and sing every morning in the shower. I have a beautiful home, play golf every day, and enjoy my businesses. My daughter graduated college last year—she is beautiful, talented, and wonderful, a tribute, I think, to her father and I being the kind of parents we had hoped to be.

"By most accounts, I'm going against the odds: I am single, a woman, and black. But I am happy with my two dogs, and I have a good life.

"I'm lucky in that I was dealt good genes—my mother is beautiful—and I did the best with what I had. That I was on the cover of *Vogue* was extraordinary. The fact that I broke the color barrier, that I would be this person in history whose black face and skin are finally accepted as a symbol of beauty in America, was a profound and life-changing experience. I am honored that it paved the way for others, and I am grateful that it helped afford me the life I now have.

{ "To me, true beauty is about mystery. There's something very sexy about it." }

"Being from a lower-middle-class black family, I knew the necessity of money. Modeling was simply a means to that end. I understood this best when I got my first check. It was right after my freshman year at Northeastern; I got paid $300. My eyes nearly popped out of my head. Until then, I'd earned $17 to $28 a week as a lifeguard at my local YWCA.

"I returned to college—I was a criminal justice major—but continued modeling and eventually transferred to Brooklyn College. By then, I knew my career wasn't going to be law, but in the arts. So, in addition to modeling, I studied acting with Lee Strasberg. In 1978, I starred opposite Michael Caine in *Ashanti*.

"In my business, unfortunately, there is a well-known stigma about age. People look at you a certain way; in my case, no matter how old I tell them I am, they're sure I'm older. I've actually shown people my birth certificate, and people still don't believe me. So I just don't talk about it. Besides, to me, true beauty is about mystery. There's something very sexy about it. So don't talk to me about age or facelifts or any of that stuff. Who you see is who I am. Take it or leave it."

INDIANA SUE ▷ Just before turning 50, explorer extraordinaire Sue Hendrickson built a home on an island off Honduras. It is the first house she's actually called her own since childhood. After spending more than 30 years traveling the globe searching for "treasure"—both underwater and underground—Hendrickson was used to sleeping on boats, in tents, and under the stars. But having a permanent dwelling has not transformed her into a permanent dweller.

Raised in Indiana, Hendrickson is a self-taught fossil hunter. Her underwater adventures have helped unearth the largest known shark's tooth, Napoleon's lost fleet, and Cleopatra's royal quarters. Her proudest moment occurred when she was 40, soon after she had discovered the largest, most complete *Tyrannosaurus rex* fossil skeleton ever found. "I always wanted children," says Hendrickson, "but I was constantly diving or digging in various parts of the world and never got around to it. So when I found this *T. rex*, I told everybody, 'This is my baby.'"

In reality, it took a court battle to determine the true owner of the 65-million-year-old find. Many claimants stepped forward, including the owner of the land in South Dakota on which the *T. rex* was found. In 1997, a judge ordered that the rare find be sold at auction. With a bid of more than $8 million, Chicago's Field Museum took home the prize, dubbed "Sue" in honor of the woman who discovered her.

A "shy nerd" who dropped out of high school in her senior year because "I was bored," Hendrickson spent much of her life diving for tropical fish and lobsters to earn money. She admits the path she's taken was a risky one, and she does not want to be "a poster child" for what high school dropouts can accomplish. A voracious reader who often finishes a book a day, she is an expert in both paleontology and marine archaeology, with an honorary Ph.D. from the University of Illinois. "I'm a reader, an investigator, and an inquirer who believes wholeheartedly in education," she says.

{ "One day, I'll probably be considered the ancient person who looks for ancient things." }

Far from becoming rich by exploring, Hendrickson donates the money she earns from deep sea dives to an education fund that benefits children from Peru, Honduras, and the Dominican Republic, saying "I've lived a charmed life; this is my way of giving back."

The only thought Hendrickson ever gave to being middle-aged occurred when she was much younger. "I thought age would bring the desire to do less rigorous work," she laughs. It hasn't happened. "Fieldwork is extremely taxing, but I can't stop. I'm addicted. One day, I'll probably be considered 'the ancient person who looks for ancient things.'"

sue

Occupation:
Archaeologist,
Paleontologist

Born:
December 2, 1949

Hendrickson

SIDMEL

ESTES-SUMPTER

Occupation:
TV Producer
Born:
November 27, 1954

MY BODY, MYSELF ▷ "I never thought I'd be heading into 50 at this size," says Sidmel Estes-Sumpter. Although she had tried "every diet on the market," she weighed 345 pounds. Four years ago, when her doctor told her she'd die if she didn't lose weight, the Fox television producer lost 130 pounds after undergoing gastric bypass surgery.

"I'd spent most of my life frustrated by diets—losing weight, then gaining it all back plus some. Many nights, I cried myself to sleep, cringing at the humiliations I'd suffered at the hands of people who didn't understand that morbid obesity is a disease."

When Estes-Sumpter was 26, her mother died from complications of alcoholism. A doctor warned her and her brother of what he believed might be a genetic predisposition to addiction. All the same, "I never thought of food as an addiction," she explains.

After losing her mother, Estes-Sumpter grew up fast. She excelled in school, eventually earning a graduate degree in journalism from Northwestern University. She was determined to succeed at everything, including a relationship. At 330 pounds, she met the love of her life; today she has been married for 18 years to a man she jokingly says belongs to what she calls BWLBW: Brothers Who Love Big Women. But it was her two sons, now 12 and 7, who were the catalyst for her lifesaving surgery.

{ "Many nights, I cried myself to sleep, cringing at the humiliations I'd suffered." }

"I was showing the doctor a picture of my boys, and he said, 'If that isn't reason enough to lose weight, I don't know what is.' He meant that I might not live to see them grown." Estes-Sumpter began to research her condition. She found that the best method for long-term weight control for morbid obesity is surgery. On July 6, 1999, she checked into the hospital.

"It was my independence day—the last barrier," she says. "I'd conquered the challenges of being a woman and being African-American. Now, I've conquered the challenge of being overweight." Since her operation, the 5'7" Estes-Sumpter has gone from a size 32 to a size 14. The surgery was relatively easy; after a couple of days in the hospital, she was able to recover at home, returning to work within three weeks.

For her fiftieth birthday, the woman who shops "for stylish Capri pants and still can't believe it" dreams of surgery to remove excess skin left from the weight loss. Even without that, she says, "I'm looking forward to the half-century mark and planning the second half of my life. Had I not lost the weight, I don't know if I'd be thinking this way—or even be here to think it."

CYBILL

Occupation:
Actress, Model
Born:
February 18, 1950

SHEPHERD

{Mississippi Queen} Over the past 30 years, Cybill Shepherd has been a beauty queen, a model, a movie star, a television and stage actress, a talk show host, a political activist, an author, and a singer. She's also the mother of three: Clementine, 22, and twins Ariel and Zachariah, 14. One of the country's first supermodels, she was on the cover of *Glamour* magazine five times in one year, and, at the age of 21, she landed a starring role in her first film,

The Last Picture Show. She's had two hit television series—*Moonlighting* and *Cybill*—and has won four Golden Globes for Best Actress. Last year, she released her seventh album, *Live at the Cinegrill.* Twice divorced, she's currently single.

question: Is it true you once turned down a ring from Elvis?

answer: It wasn't that kind of ring [an engagement ring]. It was a gaudy, hideous thing. I never really liked jewelry, especially elaborate jewelry, so I thanked him for the gesture and didn't take it. He also offered me pills, which I flushed down the toilet. Men were always trying to give me drugs, I think, so I'd have sex with them. But I never liked drugs. Sex is another story.

question: In your autobiography, *Cybill Disobedience,* you talk a lot about your sexual escapades—but also about your early days in the church and singing in the choir. With that kind of foundation, were you ever conflicted?

answer: I had a deep connection with my childhood Episcopal church and knew I shouldn't be sexual until marriage. But I hit puberty when birth control pills came out. It was also during the "make love, not war" era. Therapy at 40 finally helped me sort it out.

question: How have your attitudes about sex changed now that you're over 50?

answer: I love sex more than ever, but now that I'm older, I'm much less desperate. I'm single, and I date—just date. I don't have to have sex with anybody. Being sexual is part of being healthy, and I'm finding new ways to enjoy life when by myself. The simple act of lighting candles and enjoying them while you're alone, for example, can also bring enormous pleasure.

question: Do you dread menopause and getting older?

answer: Being past childbearing age is thrilling, because now is a time to rebirth myself. We have to find new ways to love our aging bodies and redefine what's really important to us. For some reason, we fear being "invisible" at this age—but we're not. People pretend we're invisible because we're more threatening. But we're free to be who we are. Personally, I'm looking forward to spending more time with my children.

question: Wasn't your character on *Cybill* one of the first to broach the subject of menopause?

answer: Yes. I was really proud of that. We were also the first to say "period" and "cervix" in prime time. The network balked at "vagina," but "labia" got through. They got a lot of calls about it.

question: Did people say it was a sin?

answer: How could that be? The ultimate sin is being boring.

"We have to find new ways to love our aging bodies and redefine what's really important to us."

BALANCING ACT ▷ In the lead role in *Peter Pan*, former Olympic gymnast Cathy Rigby logged a lot of frequent flyer miles. She starred in national tours of J. M. Barrie's classic childhood tale for more than four years; her performance on Broadway earned her a Tony nomination in 1991. She and husband Tom McCoy own McCoy/Rigby Enterprises, which mounts stage productions for California's La Mirada Theater. This year, they will produce *Camelot* and *Jesus Christ Superstar* for national tours. Rigby has four children, ranging in age from 16 to 26.

question: Well, here it is: the Big Five-O. Are you ready for what 50 might bring?

answer: To tell the truth, I haven't even thought about being 50. I'm happier and more successful than I've ever been and have a sense of confidence and freedom that I think only comes with age. Professionally, I only do what I want to do, and I don't get nervous like I used to. When you start thinking you're only as good as your last success or your last medal, you become like a hamster on a treadmill.

question: Was this a feeling that came about gradually, or was there an event attached to it?

answer: I was really anxious about life when I was in my forties. I desperately wanted another baby, and suffered two miscarriages at 42 and 43. Then, when I was 45, I got that baby—only it was a grandbaby. It was so strange; I had never thought of myself as a grandmother. But oh, is

{ "I had never thought of myself as a grandmother. But oh, is it wonderful! You see that the cycle of life goes on." }

it wonderful! You see that the cycle of life goes on, and it is, in a way, a relief. You can relax.

question: So you found it difficult to relax when you were younger?

answer: By age 20, I was absolutely burned out from my years as a gymnast. I had no passion left, no direction—so I spent the next 20 years reading every self-help book I could get my hands on. I also battled an eating disorder for 12 years.

question: How did you resolve that illness?

answer: I got divorced—not that my first husband was the cause, but I remarried a completely different kind of person, who instilled in me the importance of self-expression. I'd grown up with a raging alcoholic father—he's fine now—and a mother who never complained. When I was away from home, I spent most of my time with a coach who was exceedingly controlling. My husband said he wanted to hear my voice in everything, and he encouraged me to express myself. Now, he believes he's created a monster, but he loves the monster too.

question: One last question: Did Peter Pan ever get hot flashes?

answer: No, but at one point I went on estrogen because I got so cranky. It helped a lot.

CATHY

RIGBY

Occupation:
Gymnast, Actress
Born:
December 12, 1952

cristina

Occupation:
TV Host
Born:
January 29, 1948

saraLeGui

BREAKING SILENCES ▷ Cristina Saralegui, host and executive producer of Univision's *El Show de Cristina*, has been called "Oprah with salsa." With an international audience of 100 million, her show is the number one talk show on Spanish-language television.

question: You've introduced subjects on your TV show that have never before been discussed in the Latino community. Were you on a mission?

answer: In 1989, Latinos didn't mention homosexuality. Being gay was like being a mass murderer. Latino women hadn't talked about hot flashes; when I have them on the air, I fan myself. These days, I am "Our Lady of Our Menopause"—something my mother never, ever told me about. It was a conspiracy, a secret. People had fear about these issues. They didn't have information, and information is power. I consider myself a warrior of the armies of the light.

{ "After menopause, you can do what you want. Until then, you are doing what's expected of you." }

question: Is this your biggest accomplishment?

answer: Having children and realizing my purpose in life is to be well-rounded—those are my greatest achievements. I've seen friends totally devoted to their careers, and how messed up their children's lives become. I made sure my kids know me. When you retire at 65, you can't put your arms around a career and hug it.

question: At one time, your network suggested diction lessons to make your accent less Cuban—but you refused to toy with your heritage. Did the network suggest your facelift?

answer: I got a facelift at 44 because the television lights were getting so bright I couldn't see and my face was so hot you could fry an egg on it. The lighting people were saying, "Bring out the old lady lights." I was like a piece of furniture to them. So I had a facelift, and it changed my life. I started losing weight. I changed my wardrobe. I felt beautiful.

question: Even before your facelift, you attracted a younger husband. Can you tell us about that?

answer: We met when I was 36 and he was a 24-year-old bass player with Miami Sound Machine. It was "hate at first sight," because I was this tough, aggressive professional woman. But one night, he saw me cry and realized I was vulnerable. We talked. I fell hard. He sucked my toes. I fell even harder. Until him, I didn't believe in love. My advice: Find a man who'll suck your toes.

question: Does menopause interfere with this thinking?

answer: Are you kidding? It's harder being younger than older. After menopause, you can do what you want. Until then, you are doing what's expected of you. You go over a hump, but after that you get your zeal back and nothing can stop you. You go from survival to mastery.

FAITH

Occupation:
Educator, Mentor
Born:
September 7, 1948

SPOTTED eagle

{Role Model} A member of the Ihanktonwan band of Nakota/Dakota Indians (commonly called the Sioux), Faith Spotted Eagle lives on the Rosebud Reservation in Mission, South Dakota. While an undergraduate at American University, she interned for Senator George McGovern of South

Dakota. Later she received a master's degree in counseling from the University of South Dakota. In the Seventies, she helped found the White Buffalo Calf Woman Society, a women's shelter on the Rosebud Reservation. In 1994, she revived the Braveheart Women's Society, which calls on tribal grandmothers to help restore fading traditions. She and her husband, Brian Collins, a lawyer and tribal judge, have a daughter, Brook, 21, and a son, Kip, 25.

"Traditionally, one of the greatest honors a woman can have in our tribe is to be a *wakanka*— an 'old lady.' It is an elevated place of respect. I learned about it from my grandmother, who lived to be 104 and helped raise me. Her teachings provided me with a road map on how to live and guided me to the position of leadership I now have. We are trying to pass down the concept to our young women today, since what is missing among them is a sense of worthiness and self-respect.

"These days the young girls on our reservation have so many more problems. They haven't had the intergenerational interaction that I did. That is what the Braveheart Women's Society is trying to provide.

"It was eight years ago that my four sisters and I began talking about how we could re-create some of the customs we were lonesome for. We began to pray for direction, and it was decided we should try showing the young Indian girls how to be better mothers. We took 25 girls up into the mountains for a retreat, to teach them. Instead, they taught us. We discovered that they couldn't become better mothers until they first rectified the trauma of not feeling good about themselves. To do this, they have to recall their spirits, to recover from things like alcoholism, racism, rape, and the premature and accidental deaths of loved ones. The experience was like a rebirth. Now we go into the mountains once a year, with one of the grandmothers giving guidance.

"We also have reinstituted Isna Ti Awica Dowan—the coming-of-age ceremony for girls. When they begin their menses, we teach them the sacredness of their bodies. Many of our sacred rites

"NOW THAT I am OLDER, I KNOW I am more

were forbidden by law until 1978, when the Indian Religious Freedom Act was passed. Many had gone underground or faded away. Now we are bringing them back.

"The grandmothers from long ago have seen what we are doing, and they are so happy this is happening. Some of the first girls to go on retreat have grown up, and we see the difference. For some it takes a long time, but change can happen. Our group really has affected girls' lives.

"Now that I am older, I know I am more respected by my people than I would be in the Euro-white world. I didn't even think about 50. Thirty was difficult, because I wanted another child but questioned whether or not it would be OK when the world was so violent. But I had my second child, my daughter, and I am grateful because I have learned so many things from her."

respected BY MY PEOPLE THAN I WOULD BE IN THE EURO-WHITE WORLD.

a novel prosecutor ▷ "I was 12 the first time I heard the word 'rape,'" says

Linda Fairstein, recalling the afternoon her father—a doctor and mystery lover—took her to see the classic film *Anatomy of a Murder.* "Little did I know the enormous impact that one word would have on my life. It was strange, because at the time, it just wasn't in people's vocabulary."

Today, the word is part of her professional lexicon—in her role as chief of the Manhattan Sex Crimes Prosecution Unit and also as the author of five books that deal with the topic. One of the first women to prosecute sex crimes for the Manhattan District Attorney, Fairstein joined that office in 1972 after graduating from the University of Virginia law school, where she had been one of 12 women in a class of 320. Even today, she vividly remembers the first rape victim she ever interviewed.

"She was 14; I was 26," she says. "It was gut-wrenching. The victim had been raped at knifepoint, and while I tried to keep a professional perspective, it was intensely emotional. I took it home with me for days." The young woman kept in touch with Fairstein for several years, as do many rape victims she's interviewed.

"The personal stories I hear are no less agonizing now than they were when I started," she says. "The day I'm no longer affected by them will be the day I leave."

{ "The personal stories I hear are no less agonizing now than they were when I started." }

To help the public better understand what she calls "this horrendous, violent crime," Fairstein writes books. One is nonfiction; the rest are novels whose protagonist, the head of a sex crimes unit, seems "suspiciously familiar" to Fairstein's family and friends. "Society still can't deal with the realities of rape," she explains. "Hopefully, through my fictional characters, people can get the messages that will ultimately bring about change."

Finding time to write is a challenge. "Well, my husband will tell you I do it on 'his time'— vacations and weekends—but he never complains," Fairstein laughs. Justin Feldman, her husband, is 28 years her senior, but "he's got more energy than I do," she says. The couple have no children and no regrets: "When would there be time?" she asks.

On her fiftieth birthday, Fairstein was in a hospital having elective surgery on her hand. "I'd just had my second novel published; it was about a murder set in a hospital," she says. "And there I was. I had to laugh—I couldn't believe at this point in life that I was able to have two jobs that meant so much to me. Sometimes I stop and reflect on how absolutely, truly lucky I am."

LINDA

FAIRSTEIN

Occupation:
AIDS Activist
Born:
June 7, 1947

BEVERLY

MOSLEY

ONE DAY AT A TIME ▷ Ten years ago, at the age of 45, Beverly Mosley was diagnosed with HIV. She had unknowingly contracted the disease from her fiancé, who, as she would eventually learn, was bisexual. At the time of her diagnosis, Mosley had just broken off the engagement and landed a new job. She was happy with life after years of struggling.

It had been a long road. By 18, Mosley was married with two daughters. At 20, when the marriage ended, she began living in the fast lane, hanging out with the wrong crowd. At 25, when a brief second marriage broke up, she moved to Los Angeles, determined to change her life. Later, while working as a receptionist for a law firm, she became acquainted with a man who worked in her building, and a friendship developed. When Mosley changed jobs, a romance blossomed; 18 months later, when she was 42, the couple became engaged. It was a happy time, but one that was destined to be short-lived: Within four years, her fiancé was dead and she herself was infected. Currently an advocate for patients with AIDS, Mosley still lives in Los Angeles, where she is cofounder and board president of Women Alive, an education-focused nonprofit organization run by and for women with HIV and AIDS.

{ "There are no guarantees for any of us. But I know life does not end with HIV." }

"I didn't think about turning 50, because every second, every minute of every day I'm here is a godsend. There are no guarantees for any of us. But I know life does not end with HIV.

"Since my diagnosis, I have gained new confidence and am a much stronger person. My purpose now is to educate and to make a difference. I lead support groups, give speeches, and work on a hotline. I've traveled to Washington, D.C., to speak with researchers and attended the world AIDS conference in Geneva. I also accompany women to doctors, because HIV-infected women are generally treated differently than men. Most of the research performed today has been centered around men.

"I work with many women who got the virus from their husbands—even ministers' wives. And there are lots of older, divorced women who contract it when they start dating again. You can't be too careful; make your partner get tested and always use a condom.

"I took my AIDS test on July 4, 1992. When it came back positive, I was stunned. I cried, but then thought, 'Wait a minute, I don't have AIDS; I have the virus, and that's not a death sentence.' I believe I will be here when the cure for AIDS is discovered. But until and unless our society gets over its homophobia, we will never find one."

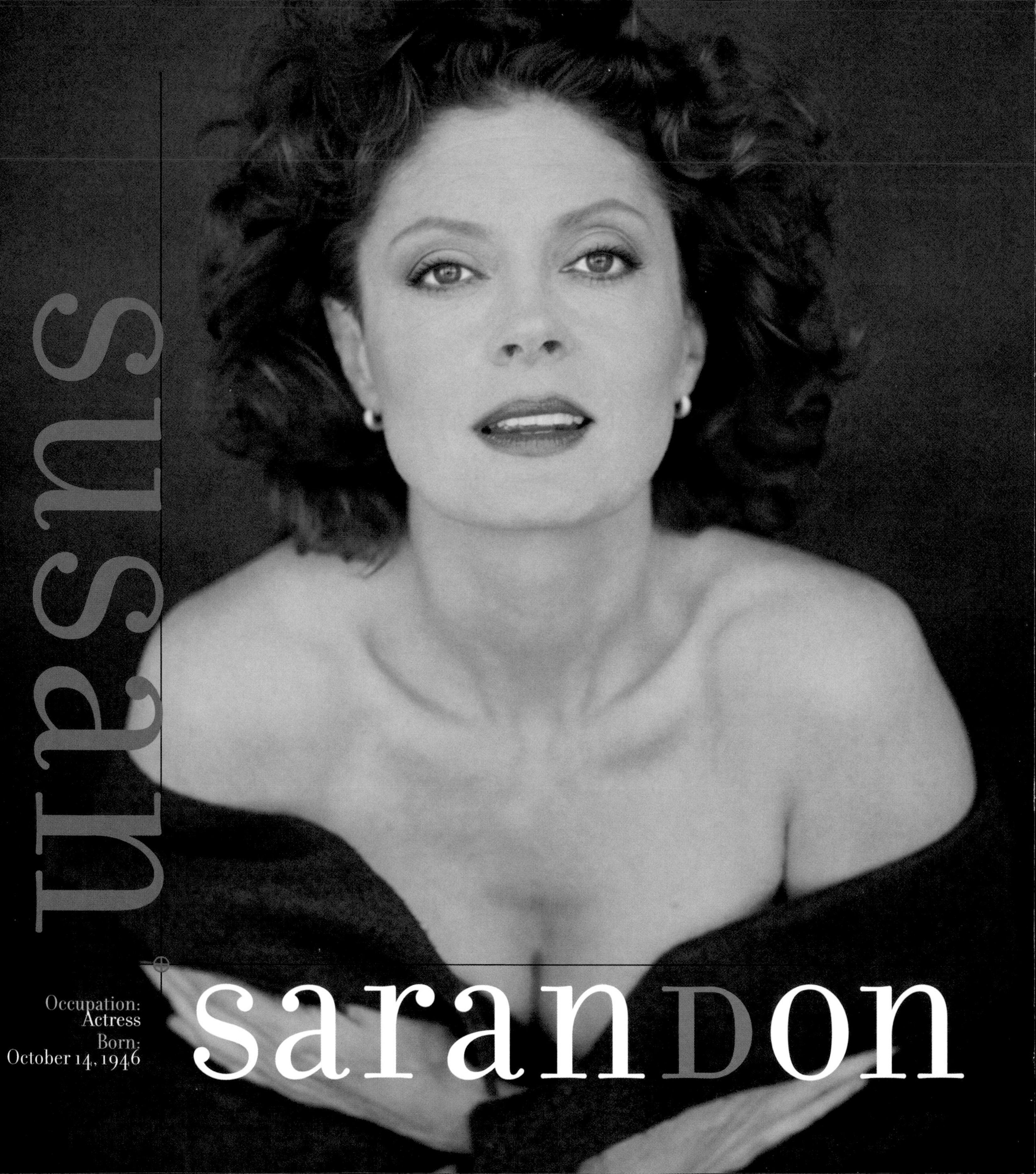

susan

Occupation:
Actress
Born:
October 14, 1946

saranDon

{Siren} "Experience is sexy," says Academy Award-winning actress Susan Sarandon. "And today, women can be sexy and 50." She should know. Though Sarandon gained acclaim early in her career with quirky films like *The Rocky Horror Picture Show* and the offbeat *Atlantic City*, she became a superstar at the age of 41 for her vibrant, sensual turn in the 1988 film *Bull Durham*. And the performance earned her more than just critical applause: During the shoot, she also won the heart of costar Tim Robbins, 12 years her junior. Today, Robbins has been her partner for 14 years and is the

THE BEAUTY AND *MYSTERY* **OF THIS** LIFE **IS NOT IN ARRIVING AT**

father of her two sons, Jack, 13, and Miles, 10. (Sarandon also has a 17-year-old daughter, Eva, whose father is the Italian director Franco Amurri.) "Motherhood," she laughs, "is the sexiest thing of all!"

Sarandon, who was born in New York City, was raised in New Jersey as the oldest of nine children. She knows what it means to blossom in midlife, and today is known mainly for roles she played when she was past 40. From her gritty star turn in *Thelma and Louise* (1991) to her tender performance as the mother of four girls in 1994's *Little Women*, she has demonstrated a remarkable range that has earned her five Academy Award nominations, culminating in a Best Actress award in 1996 for her role (opposite Sean Penn) as Sister Helen Prejean in *Dead Man Walking*, a film that was produced and directed by Robbins.

Although Sarandon studied art and drama at Washington, D.C.'s Catholic University (where, as Susan Abigail Tomalin, she met her first husband, actor Chris Sarandon), she has never formally studied acting. "I just started going on auditions and got everything I ever went up for," she says, a little bemused. "All the same, I never expected life to be fair or easy—so I am continually inspired by what I find. The beauty and mystery of this life is not in arriving at answers, but in the process of seeking."

And very often Sarandon goes looking—especially for causes. An impassioned activist

answers, BUT IN THE PROCESS OF seeking.

who is devoted to a wide range of issues, including AIDS awareness, abortion rights, housing for the homeless, historic-building preservation, and antiviolence, she has been known to make calls from movie sets to facilitate the delivery of food and clothing to those in need. "I've always wanted to use my celebrity before it could use me," Sarandon says. "I cannot imagine living as a celebrity and not working in the public arena to give back, to make a contribution toward a more just and humane world."

Do all of these overlapping roles become overwhelming? "When I start to feel exhausted, I remind myself how amazing it is to be here, to be a mother in my fifties to three fascinating children, to continue to jump into work I value and enjoy," Sarandon explains. "While counting my blessings, I always remember to stop for a moment and picture some of the women I've known who've influenced and inspired me—but who didn't reach 50. I gather strength from their memories."

Occupation:
Author
Born:
1947

sarah

Ban Breathnach

THE MOST ABUNDANT YEARS ▷ Gratitude, simplicity, order, harmony,

beauty, and joy: The six basic principles of Sarah Ban Breathnach's *Simple Abundance* were born out of the author's own search for happiness. Published in 1995 after 30 rejections, the book has sold more than 5 million copies. Four more best-sellers have followed. But Ban Breathnach's enormous success reaped a kind of abundance not so simple to deal with. At 50, she divorced and was once again reexamining her life. President and CEO of Simple Abundance, Inc., she lives in Maryland and is the mother of a 19-year-old daughter.

"As my fiftieth birthday approached, I was filled with dread. For me, 50 meant what my parents had made it—a complete decline. I told everyone not to mention it; I wanted no celebration. And it didn't help that I was going through a divorce.

"But I made it through that year, and, at 51, I realized I was having the time of my life. I had passion and dreams and was creating a life that was fulfilling. I'm alone and I'm OK. I won't pretend this came easily. People think I have it all figured out, but I struggle every day. I'm no one's guru.

"My daughter graduated from high school last year, and I'm especially grateful for the opportunity I've had to be with her. Had I not been alone, I wouldn't have gotten to know her in the way that I did. We're very close now.

{ "At 51, I realized I was having the time of my life. I had passion and dreams." }

"During this period, I also figured out how I want to spend my truly abundant years. I've bought a cottage in England, where I hope to raise rare sheep and have an herb garden. My process of achieving simple abundance continues. It's not about money, but about the richness life can give you when you know what your priorities are. My greatest challenge is holding on to who I am and not being molded into other people's expectations. When *Simple Abundance* was published, I was astonished to learn people had parameters for what my life should be.

"My fifties also brought a new awareness of my physical being. I exercise and eat properly. And for the very first time, I actually see myself as beautiful. When a photographer offered to take my picture in the persona of whoever I wished to be, the result—modeled after a John Singer Sargent painting—was a reflection of my romantic self. It's a part of me I pushed down for a long time, and it is far from the Birkenstock image many have projected onto me.

"I have learned these past few years that you can't place security over happiness. I look forward to creating my most abundant years living out who I truly am, and doing it with gratitude."

HOTTer THan ever ▷

She's a grandmother, but Donna Summer is still hot stuff. More than 25 years after she first moaned her infamous 17-minute "Love to Love You Baby," the five-time Grammy winner is touring the globe, selling out concerts before multigenerational crowds. The so-called queen of disco got her start at 8, when she sang her first solo in church. At 18, she was in the German production of *Hair.* While in Europe, she met her first husband, actor Helmut Sommer, and had a daughter, Mimi, now 29. By 1975, she was an international star. The following year, she and Sommer divorced; she kept his name but changed the spelling. By 1979, she had two Grammys. Fame, money, romance—Summer had it all.

Then, in the mid-Eighties, disco took a dive. Summer released moderately successful gospel albums and a few rock singles. Torn between genres, she retreated to family life, began painting seriously, and wrote songs with second husband Bruce Sudano. She and Sudano have two children—Brooklyn, 21, and Amanda Grace, 20. And recently her career has revived: When she's not touring, she records albums and is working on a Broadway musical about her life. With homes in Nashville and New York, Summer spends as much time as she can with granddaughters Vienna and Savannah.

"I loved turning 50—if I hadn't really lived, then maybe I would feel differently. I have a sense of completeness. I've had and still have the opportunity to express myself in ways others haven't. It feels great at this stage to be able to pack stadiums. I tried to maintain a skeletal career while I raised my children and didn't court the media because I wanted my privacy. I figured when the time was right, I could do a career again, and that's what I'm in the process of doing.

"I still boogie. I dance by myself in the house whenever I feel the urge. I'm a joyful person. I can get ecstatic over a flower blooming. I'm a very simple person: I don't need a mansion, and I don't go to a lot of parties.

"I used to have an impending sense of doom, always looking to the outside to find happiness. At one point, I felt I had sold my soul and didn't know who I was anymore. I became severely depressed. I thought God couldn't love me. But I prayed and asked for forgiveness, and that's all it took. I am most grateful for getting back on track in my spiritual life.

"People still refer to me as 'the queen of disco,' but I'm not sure what that means anymore. I am simply the 'empress of myself,' and that's as good as it gets—to be who I am and to be the best I can be at that."

> { "People still refer to me as 'the queen of disco,' but I'm not sure what that means anymore." }

Donna

summer

Occupation:
Musician
Born:
December 31, 1948

Index

PHOTOGRAPHY CREDITS

Index

more®

the one magazine that understands who you are, where you are, and what you're feeling at this wonderful stage in life!

---

rush!
free-yearrequest

---

rush!
free-giftrequest